The Poetry of John Tyndall

COMPARATIVE LITERATURE AND CULTURE

Series Editors
TIMOTHY MATHEWS AND FLORIAN MUSSGNUG

Comparative Literature and Culture explores new creative and critical perspectives on literature, art and culture. Contributions offer a comparative, cross-cultural and interdisciplinary focus, showcasing exploratory research in literary and cultural theory and history, material and visual cultures, and reception studies. The series is also interested in language-based research, particularly the changing role of national and minority languages and cultures, and includes within its publications the annual proceedings of the 'Hermes Consortium for Literary and Cultural Studies'.

Timothy Mathews is Emeritus Professor of French and Comparative Criticism, UCL.

Florian Mussgnug is Reader in Italian and Comparative Literature, UCL.

The Poetry of John Tyndall

Edited by
Roland Jackson, Nicola Jackson and Daniel Brown

UCLPRESS

First published in 2020 by
UCL Press
University College London
Gower Street
London WC1E 6BT

Available to download free: www.uclpress.co.uk

A CIP catalogue record for this book is available from The British Library.

ISBN: 978-1-78735-912-3 (Hbk.)
ISBN: 978-1-78735-911-6 (Pbk.)
ISBN: 978-1-78735-910-9 (PDF)
ISBN: 978-1-78735-913-0 (epub)
ISBN: 978-1-78735-914-7 (mobi)
DOI: https://doi.org/10.14324/111.9781787359109

Frontispiece: Chalk drawing of John Tyndall c.1850, at the time he was writing many of these poems. Courtesy of the Royal Institution of Great Britain.

Contents

Notes on contributors

Roland Jackson is a historian and scientist, concentrating on the history, policy and ethics of science and technology. He has recently published a biography of John Tyndall, *The Ascent of John Tyndall* (OUP, 2018), and is one of the three general editors of the Tyndall Correspondence Project, which is publishing Tyndall's extant correspondence in 20 volumes with Pittsburgh University Press. He was previously Chief Executive of the British Science Association, and Head of the Science Museum. He is currently a Research Associate in the Department of Science and Technology Studies at UCL, and a Visiting Fellow and Trustee of the Royal Institution.

Nicola Jackson has a DPhil in behavioural neuroscience from Oxford University and has worked in Further Education colleges. In 2016–18 she completed an MA in Writing Poetry at Newcastle University and the Poetry School, London. She has published a range of research papers and contributed to numerous public reports. Her poetry is published in journals and newspapers, and her poetry collection *Difficult Women* won the Geoff Stevens Memorial Prize in 2018.

Daniel Brown has written on nineteenth-century physics and literature studies in his book *Hopkins' Idealism: Philosophy, Physics, Poetry* (OUP, 1997) and has since helped to develop this field in further writings, principally in the CUP title *The Poetry of Victorian Scientists: Style, Science and Nonsense* (2013), the first book-length study of such poetry. He is currently writing a study that explores the consequences of women's exclusion from Victorian professional science as they are disclosed by poetry written by both Victorian scientists and women themselves.

Acknowledgements

We offer particular thanks to The Royal Institution of Great Britain for giving us access to the previously unpublished manuscript poems and enabling us to publish them. Professor Frank James, formerly Head of Collections and Heritage, has been highly encouraging and supportive, and we thank also Charlotte New and Jane Harrison for their unflagging work in making the archives accessible to us. We are grateful to two anonymous referees, who gave us constructive feedback which was most helpful in our final revisions.

We have benefited greatly from all the efforts of publishing *The Correspondence of John Tyndall*, of which one of us (Roland Jackson) is a general editor, and thank Professor Bernard Lightman and all those who have contributed to the project. We thank Pittsburgh University Press for permission to use endnotes from the handful of poems that have been published in the Tyndall correspondence.

It has been a pleasure to work with UCL Press. We thank Chris Penfold, Jaimee Biggins, Margie Coughlin, Niranjana Anand, Liron Gilenberg, Lucy Hall, Servis Filmsetting and any others behind the scenes of whom we are unaware.

Editorial principles and abbreviations

Most of the poems published in this book exist only in handwritten manuscript form. In the few cases where there are contemporarily printed versions, we have published those versions here, with references to any further primary sources, including drafts. Where there are several drafts of an individual poem, including overlapping drafts, we have taken an editorial decision about where to start and end the version published here, commenting and quoting in an endnote if there are alternative lines in drafts that seem particularly significant. We have integrated all Tyndall's own editorial drafting changes – such as crossings-out, insertions and any other alterations – to give a single reading. However, we have lodged our detailed raw transcripts with the Royal Institution, so that scholars who wish to follow up any particular poems may do so with more ease. About half the poems were not given specific titles by Tyndall, and in those cases a title is shown in brackets; we have generally taken the first few words or first line of the poem as this title. Dates that are uncertain are given in italics. Endnotes for the poems follow the broad strategy used for the letters being published in *The Correspondence of John Tyndall*. They offer contextual factual information about people, places and events in Tyndall's life but do not extend to commentary on the poetry itself. That broader analysis and collection of collaborative insights we leave to the introductory essay, which we hope offers fruitful avenues for scholars to explore further should they so wish.

RI MS	The Royal Institution of Great Britain, London, manuscript source.
BL Add MS	British Library, London, manuscript source.
TC1	Cantor, Geoffrey and Gowan Dawson (eds). 2016. *The Correspondence of John Tyndall*, vol. 1. Pittsburgh: Pittsburgh University Press.
TC2	Baldwin, Melinda and Janet Browne (eds). 2016. *The Correspondence of John Tyndall*, vol. 2. Pittsburgh: Pittsburgh University Press.

Poetry in context

Introduction

In 1864, when he was in his early 40s, the sceptical John Tyndall, physicist and emerging public intellectual, attended a séance. He wrote an amusing account of the episode in *The Reader* magazine, in which he reported that the spirits had dubbed him 'The Poet of Science'.[1] In this guise he preceded his friend Alfred Tennyson, who was not so described until after his death.[2] Yet the meaning of 'poet' here needs qualifying. It was the vivid language Tyndall used in his lectures and books that gave him this status, not least in his writings about mountains and landscape. As W. T. Jeans wrote in 1887: 'I do not know that he has ever written poetry, but he is certainly a poet in the fire of his imagination and in his love for all the forms of natural beauty.'[3] Few people were aware that Tyndall did indeed write poetry.

In this book we publish for the first time all Tyndall's extant poetry. The volume consists of 76 poems and significant fragments. While they were written throughout his lifetime, the majority date from the 1840s and 1850s, when Tyndall was in his 20s and 30s. To introduce this collection, we explore what the poems can tell us about: Tyndall himself; his values and beliefs; the role of poetry for him and his wider circle; and, more broadly, the relationship between the scientific and poetic imaginations, and wider questions of the nature and purpose of poetry in relation to science and religion in the nineteenth century.

Tyndall's poems fall into several categories, from early political statements, through explorations of personal relationships, to deep reflections on Nature and the universe. There are some powerful and sensitive pieces. Tyndall was realistic about his own talents, writing to Thomas Henry Huxley in 1852:

> It is said that every son of Adam has some spark of poetic sentiment in him, and that what distinguishes the poet proper from other men is the faculty of being able to tell you what he and all feel. Were I a poet (and I know not whether to upbraid or bless the gods for not making me one) I should sit down with delight to gather from birds and blossoms their prettiest imagery, and from the May its sunshine and odours into one sweet bouquet to present to you.[4]

Tyndall's poetry reveals much about him and about the nature and purpose of poetry during his lifetime. He is currently the focus of much scholarly interest,[5] as are the connections between science, poetry and wider literature in the nineteenth century.[6] This hitherto neglected, largely unpublished body of work offers unique insights into Tyndall himself and these broader connections.

Tyndall in context

Tyndall was for his contemporaries the most celebrated of scientific self-made men, and he remains the foremost example of this Victorian type. Like his close friend and ally Huxley, Tyndall incarnates the meritocratic professional science of the generation that followed the 'gentlemen' who founded the British Association for the Advancement of Science (BAAS) in 1831.[7] The son of a failed schoolmaster, Huxley came to a career in biology through working as a ship's surgeon on *HMS Rattlesnake* during the late 1840s, while Tyndall, the son of a shoemaker and leather dealer from Carlow, came to science after working as a draughtsman and surveying assistant for the Irish and then the English Ordnance Survey, for railway companies and a brief stint as a teacher of mathematics and surveying at Queenwood College in Hampshire. In 1848 he travelled with his colleague from Queenwood, Edward Frankland to the University of Marburg, where for the following two years he studied chemistry, experimental physics and mathematics under Robert Bunsen, Hermann Knoblauch and Friedrich Stegmann, qualifying for his doctorate without any prior university education. Returning to England in 1851, he was elected a Fellow of the Royal Society a year later, and in 1853 he was appointed Professor of Natural Philosophy at the Royal Institution, a position he kept until he retired in 1887.

Tyndall and Huxley, like such peers as Frankland and Thomas Archer Hirst, gained and sustained careers in science through merit and discipline, bolstered by ambition and political astuteness. These instances of social mobility propelled by scientific merit have become unremarkable, making it easy to lose sight of the novelty and achievement of such pioneering examples as Tyndall and Huxley. The British Association had been established as a reforming alternative to the Royal Society, which Charles Babbage had charged with retaining and retarding British science as an aristocratic demesne. Most of the men who formed the BAAS were liberal Christians who incorporated natural theology into their work. Tyndall and Huxley represented the next generation, many of whom would challenge this outlook. But not all. The contemporary man of science whose poetry is one of the most studied, James Clerk Maxwell, had profound religious beliefs. As we shall see, the one poem of his that Tyndall sent privately to Maxwell offers an intriguing glimpse into their relationship. In addition to their religious differences, the contrast in both their outlooks on natural philosophy and in their class origins set the background for their relationship and for some of the ways in which Tyndall later used poetry in his writings. Tyndall and Maxwell and their respective associates all met at the annual BAAS meetings. Over time, Maxwell and his so-called 'North British' group, typically Scots Presbyterian and Cambridge Mathematical Tripos wranglers, were pitched against Tyndall, Huxley and their 'Metropolitans', London-based and agnostic. Their contest is usually described as a series of metaphysical and methodological oppositions between idealism and materialism, Christian belief and agnosticism, esoteric mathematical and public-facing demonstrative science practices.

Class assumptions also determined the ways in which natural philosophy was taught and could progress in England. The experimental physics that Tyndall studied at Marburg, and which his peer Maxwell undertook at Edinburgh in the late 1840s, was disdained by the English universities as a form of manual labour. Purely theoretical physics was taught through the Mathematical Tripos degree at Cambridge and was only supplemented by experimental physics in 1871, when Maxwell became the first Cavendish professor, overseeing the construction of what would become the Cavendish Laboratory and the introduction of the new course. Nevertheless, by this time professional physics had been resolutely established as a mathematical discipline, with Maxwell's friends and colleagues William Thomson and Peter Guthrie Tait having systematised energy physics mathematically in their 1867 *Treatise on Natural Philosophy*. Physics that was not grounded in advanced mathematics, such as that practised by Tyndall and presented in his research papers and lecture demonstrations at the Royal Institution, was stigmatised by Maxwell and his peers. Tyndall had studied at a German university, not at Cambridge, Oxford or Edinburgh, with their classical and religious underpinnings. In addition, the lectures that enthralled Tyndall's London society audiences were criticised for foregrounding style over content, displaying a distracting theatricality or showy empiricism, which overshadowed conceptual understanding and hence mathematics.

The class position of such figures as Maxwell was assured by the readily recognisable cultural capital he acquired through a classical education. While it is often highlighted by the classical allusions and references that Maxwell and others made in the poetry they wrote for their fellow men of science, the genre of verse was shaped by more popular models. The classical learning of Maxwell and his peers marks a continuity with the earlier aristocratic science of the Royal Society, whereas the more demotic cultural capital of figures who had not had such educational opportunities, such as Tyndall and Huxley, was a new element that still tends to go unrecognised, despite its decisive influence in shaping the culture of Victorian professional science. It too is disclosed by poetry by such men of science. The natural historian Edward Forbes, Huxley's friend and mentor, established the forms for BAAS poetry and the mores around its recitation in 1839, when he and some friends, forsaking the official dinner in favour of a meal at a local tavern, began the playful 'Red Lion Club'.

Many of the Anglican 'Gentlemen of Science', who founded the BAAS as a reforming alternative to the Royal Society, nevertheless considered aristocratic patronage necessary for the survival of the association. They accordingly held lavish formal dinners at the annual meetings, which many younger men of science of merit, but little means, did not enjoy. At the 1839 Birmingham meeting of the BAAS a breakaway group of young geologists and palaeontologists, led by Forbes, opted instead for informal dinners at a local tavern, The Red Lion, an alternative to the association's official dinners that in subsequent years came to supersede them as the principal social event at the annual meetings. In a late account he wrote of the 1851 Ipswich meeting, which he attended with Tyndall, Huxley said that Forbes had established the 'Red Lion Club' at the 1839 meeting 'as a protest against Dons and Donnishness in science': 'With this object, the "Red Lions" made a point of holding a feast of Spartan simplicity and anarchic constitution, with rites of a Pantagruelistic aspect, intermingled with extremely unconventional orations and queer songs, such as only Forbes could indite, by way of counterblast to the official banquets of the Association, with their high tables and what he irreverently termed "butter-boat" speeches.'[8] The 'queer songs' that Huxley notes here refer to the drinking songs, doggerel, ballads, pastiches and other comic verses on topical themes in science and BAAS scientific culture that, starting with Forbes, members would write for and recite at the Red Lions dinners, a practice that remained central to the festivities for the remainder of the century.

Much as the simplicity of the Red Lions dinners contrasted with the pomp and formality of the early BAAS dinners, so too the verses that the Lions recited and sang drew upon popular genres, cultural forms deriving from the working- and lower middle-classes, social classes that were often dismissed as 'uncultured'. Maxwell's engagement here with the Red Lions indicates his enjoyment of these informal settings, and his poetry offers some of the best examples of the Red Lions genre, the traditions of playful, often punning and parodic, verses on the people and scientific cultures of the BAAS. While the model of poetry for the Royal Society was established by the Latin 'Ode to Newton' that Edmund Halley wrote for the first edition of the *Principia Mathematica* (1687), the verse forms that Forbes and his peers introduced speak of the modest means and meritocratic ethos of many of the rising young generation of BAAS members. Forbes was only five years older than Tyndall, who was yet to join the BAAS and attend the Lions dinners, and was also writing poetry during the 1840s. Tyndall, like Maxwell and many of their peers, came to the Red Lions club as a practised poet, ready to appreciate the forms of verse that Forbes had established for the club and which became one of its principal entertainments and traditions. The humorous camaraderie continued the jokey style that Tyndall had enjoyed with his earlier group of young male friends, expressed in poems he wrote to them at that time.

Maxwell's poetry for the Red Lions, much of which lampoons Tyndall, has received the most attention of any of the Victorian poet-physicists.[9] The present book redresses the balance, finding in Tyndall's verse a unique set of historical records that discreetly disclose the character and reveal the formative personal attitudes and cultural mores that shaped this celebrated mid-Victorian scientific and society figure. The prolific early poems can each be read to 'mark a tendency'.[10] Tyndall's verse reveals the development of the public society figure at the Royal Institution. While the ugly ducklings of the early verses quack about the prepossessions that Tyndall brings to his subsequent science and public position, 'A morning on Alp Lusgen' glides swan-like to encompass his overarching metaphysic, at once romantic and materialist, a synthesis that, finally published in 1892, a year before his death, reads as an elegiac reconciliation of the dying century's principal cosmologies.[11]

Forms and influences

Tyndall read poetry extensively throughout his life and was familiar with different poetic forms. He writes blank verse, free verse, extended couplets, ballads, acrostics, sonnets and valentines, with a clear awareness of regular rhyme schemes and metre. For example, his 1843 poem 'Suggested on hearing High Mass in Saint Wilfred's Chapel' uses carefully ordered Spenserian stanzas rhyming ababbcbcc, the first eight lines of each in pentameter and the last a hexametric alexandrine.[12] The poem is clearly carefully worked. His most polished poems, such as 'Landlord and tenant' of 1841 and 'The aerial phantazies of youth' of 1843, have a regular rhyme scheme and metre throughout.[13] Other work has metre which is at best ragged, his 1842 poem 'To Ginty' being particularly awkward metrically.[14] But it is apt for his knock-about friendship with his fellow surveyor William Ginty, rendering the sincerity of the emotion it expresses and Tyndall's concern for his friend. Nevertheless, in the main, he uses tetrameter or pentameter to controlled effect. The existence of numerous drafts of several poems evidence the care he took to craft his words. For the poem 'With cloudy head' there are perhaps five drafts,[15] overlapping with drafts of 'Dont you remember love' in which, written dramatically across the page, is a stanza beginning 'Oh! give me a lay that sparkles bright | with the gems of the radiant soul'.[16] His final poem, 'A morning on Alp Lusgen',[17] runs to many drafts and two main versions.

Half the poems which Tyndall wrote as a young man, from 1840 to 1844, can be categorised as writing about love or romance – 20 of the 40 surviving poems from that period. Other subjects include the pleasures of male companionship, his engagement with the landscape from which he took great joy and sustenance, his personal philosophy with its roots in Ireland and Irish history, and the politics of the day. Later poems focus less on romance and culminate, after an apparent gap of nearly 20 years, in 'A morning on Alp Lusgen' in 1881. Landscape also has deeper meanings; for Tyndall, it was never 'just a thrush on a branch'.[18]

Tyndall's poetic influences are many and varied. His early journal, contemporaneous to the writing of much of his poetry, refers to at least two dozen poets. Writing later to his friend, Mary Ann Coxe, he recollects that

> they bring old old days to mind when the poems of Scott and Burns were the delight of my life. When Straths, Bens, Lochs and Corries—purple heather & misty glen—constituted my ideal scenery. No note in Byron stirred me more than that:

"And wild & high the Cameron's gathering rose
The war-not[e] of Lochiel which Albyn's hills
Have heard & heard too have her highland foes
When in the noon of night that pibroch thrills."[19]

Tyndall's early biographers, basing their work on Louisa Tyndall's recollections of her late husband, describe the importance for him of Percy Bysshe Shelley, John Keats, Lord Byron, William Wordsworth, William Cowper, Thomas Campbell, Robert Burns, Ralph Waldo Emerson, Samuel Taylor Coleridge and, particularly, Alfred Tennyson. The favourite Tennyson poems were 'Sir Galahad', 'The Lotus Eaters', 'Ulysses', 'The Vision of Sin' and especially 'Oenone'.[20] He read much in his youth. Indeed his interest was probably kindled by his mother, who often recited poetry to him on their walks together. He would commit long pieces to memory to recite to himself while walking.[21]

Tyndall's letters and journals in the 1840s and 1850s, when he was writing much of his own poetry, are replete with quotations from poets. Those identified include Thomas Moore, Walter Scott, Burns, Byron, Shelley, Elizabeth Barrett Browning, John Milton, Robert Southey, Coleridge, Wordsworth, Tennyson, Emerson, Robert Blair, James Montgomery, Charles Swain, Johann Goethe, Cowper, Thomas Hood, Charles Churchill, Denis MacCarthy, Alexander Pope, Charles Mackay and Keats. Of them all, it is Byron, followed by Emerson, who is most quoted by him. Tyndall demonstrates an extensive familiarity with the canon of his day, in his capacity to pick out a line or a group of lines almost at will to emphasise a point or to create a more visual image. So, for example, in a letter to a local Irish acquaintance Burchell, describing his first sea crossing to Liverpool, Tyndall calls on Byron's *The Siege of Corinth* (1816) to intensify his description of viewing the night sky from the deck:

Who ever gazed upon them shining
And turned to earth without repining
Nor wished for wings to flee away
And mix with their eternal ray?[22]

In a letter to Ginty, Tyndall talks about poetry as an expression of individual feeling which he argues has the power to touch everyone, since he assumes people have a common nature. In so doing he builds on the following lines from Elizabeth Barrett Browning's 'An Essay on Mind' (1826):

Poetic fire, like vesta's pure and bright,
Should draw from Nature's sun its holy light
With Nature should the musing poet roam,
And steal instruction from her classic tome;
When 'neath her guidance, least inclined to err –
The ablest painter when he copies her.[23]

And in a letter to another surveying colleague Jack Tidmarsh, on hearing (an incorrect rumour) that his 'peerless' Lizzy Barton, subject of several of his own poems, had married, he appears to quote from Goethe's *Faust*, but with a touch of humour:

My peace is gone
My heart is broken![24]

Tyndall's journal contains many more examples, as he documents the events of his daily life. On 17 August 1844, on hearing that a young friend has died, he summons lines from Byron's *Don Juan* and then Thomas Carlyle's translation of Goethe's 'The Mason Lodge':

How little do we know that which we are!
How less what we may be![25]

Solemn before us
Veiled, the dark portal,
Goal of all mortal:—
Stars silent rest o'er us,
Graves under us silent.[26]

On 1 October 1846, in response to hearing on a beautiful evening the news of the stranding of *SS Great Britain* in Dandrum Bay, he misquotes Wordsworth, evidently writing it from memory:

This holy hour is quiet as a Nun
Breathless with adoration;[27]

And on 15 May 1847, Tyndall is reading Shelley's *Queen Mab* and comparing it to Byron's *Cain*. He comments that Shelley's

> irreverent attacks upon God's entity are levelled rather at the vulgar idea of the supreme than at the recognition of his abstract

existence—the latter he virtually admits. In speaking of his ideal earth he says:

> Mild was the slow necessity of death
> The tranquil spirit failed beneath its grasp
> Without a groan, almost without a fear
> Calm as a voyager to some distant land
> And full of wonder—full of hope as he.
> Again
> Even the minutest molecule of light
> That in an April sunbeam's fleeting glow
> Fulfils its destined, though invisible work,
> The Universal Spirit guides.[28]

The poetry of the materialist and atheist Shelley offers a suggestive model for the peculiar form of romantic pantheism that Tyndall develops, which is best known from his 1874 Belfast Address, and has its mature lyrical expression in his long late poem 'A morning on Alp Lusgen'. These are just a few examples of the facility with which Tyndall could call poetry to mind. He was evidently steeped in it.

The reading and reciting of poetry were a regular feature of much middle-class Victorian social life. Tyndall moved in circles where poetry was read and discussed, especially once he was established in London. He knew many poets personally in later life, including Tennyson, Robert Browning and Mackay. On a visit to Lord Ashburton's country house in Hampshire, he sat 'listening to Lady Ashburton reading Browning in the library, with Carlyle at her left and his wife, Jane, opposite'.[29] Tennyson had been there two days previously, reading 'Maud', though by the time Tyndall became friendly with Tennyson, whom he greatly admired as a poet, he would barely write any more poetry. He discussed the interpretation of poetry in his first meeting with Tennyson, in 1858. His personal proximity to such a great poet may have been a further factor in discouraging him from pursuing the art in his middle years.

Early poems

Early in his poetic forays, Tyndall wrote a series of politico-historical poems, most of which were published in the local newspaper, *The Carlow Sentinel*, in the autumn of 1841. The series starts with 'In praise of Bruen',[30] celebrating the election of a Conservative candidate in the General Election of 1841, and 'The Leighlin "Orators"—or, "The late repeal meeting"',[31] about the campaign led by Daniel O'Connell to repeal the Act of Union of 1800 between Great Britain and Ireland. Colonel Henry Bruen's electoral success at Carlow in 1841 is compared bathetically with the famous battle at Thermopylae in 480 BCE, when the Greek forces repelled a far larger army of Persian soldiers. In the subsequent 'Carlow',[32] Tyndall contrasts the serenity of the landscape,

> Sweet blissful spot! where Barrow fair and free
> Rolls liquid chrystal to the distant sea,

with the dire consequences of the conflict,

> Ere sanguine strife thy hollows had bestained
> Or friendships mourned her Sacred Courts profaned

O'Connell now is damned by his deeds, as,

> the widow's withering ban
> Shall burst in thunders o'er thee—bloody man.

A 'ban' is the uttering of a curse, a malediction expressing anger. It refers to Jane Lucretia D'Esterre, whose husband John, a member of the Dublin Corporation, was killed in a duel by O'Connell. In 'The testimonial',[33] which follows, the tone is as lofty as the mountain metaphors he uses:

> The soaring condor plumes his wing
> on Chimborazo's lofty peak.

Chimborazo is one of the highest mountains in the Andes in South America and the highest mountain in Ecuador. Tyndall references 'Ullin's hills' from *Ossian's Fingal*,[34] Robert the Bruce at the Battle of Bannockburn in 1314, and the Gorgons and Hydra, 'Lerne', from Greek mythology. The whole is a tour de force designed to demonstrate classical scholarship and his passionate views of Irish politics. The reference to 'Mononia' for the Province of Munster leads to the source poem 'Remember the Glories of Brien the Brave' in Moore's *Irish Melodies* (1821) as inspiration here. Poems of a similar ilk follow, though his 'Landlord and tenant' is more nuanced, presenting a picture of a dignified Protestant cottager,

Full seventy winter on his furrowed brow
Had spent their vehemence—yet smiling sat
Contentment there as lingers day's last beam,

praising his landlord, while a poor wretch of a (Catholic) tenant curses the absent landlord who brought his family to starvation during the potato famine.[35] Tyndall later transferred such writing to England with poems such as 'Beacon Hill',[36] still with a heroic tone:

Bidding the hardy sons of youth prepare
    To fight for home against each hostile band.

The young men of Halifax are called:

To stand in battle for those starry eyes
    To shield their bosoms pure from slight or wrong

Quite whether it was the person or morals of the young women of Halifax which needed defending is unclear. So the past has the power to inform the present for Tyndall, as social commentary with overtones of chivalry and in the defence of justice for the working man and woman.

Self-fashioning

Tyndall's extensive journals have been studied by Ian Hesketh to explore how he used them to help shape his identity as a moral and a scientific agent, in the formative period of his life between 1840 and 1855. Hesketh argues that Tyndall exemplifies the development of 'a particular scientific self that emerged in the mid-nineteenth century, whose novel claim to authority was based on a particular fusion of the ethical and the epistemological'.[37] Tyndall's journals reveal much of this self-fashioning. But not all. As Hesketh points out, Tyndall did not envisage the journal to be a record of his 'ecstasies nor yet of sufferings'. He assured himself that it would 'not be romantic'.[38] For the most part he kept to that resolution, with a few notable exceptions. So we need to look elsewhere for insights into his deeper emotions, and particularly to his poetry. Tyndall wrote directly into his journal some of the poems published here, although Hesketh does not comment on them. The majority have been found elsewhere, in separate handwritten sheets, and together they complement other writings to allow access to Tyndall's more private thoughts and feelings. Bernard Lightman's article 'Fashioning the Victorian Man of Science: Tyndall's Shifting Strategies' encompasses also the period from the 1850s onwards, when Tyndall made his career in science and as a public intellectual.[39] But this is the period in which Tyndall wrote relatively little poetry. Most of Tyndall's extant poems were written between 1840 and 1855, precisely the period of his initial self-formation. Yet even in Tyndall's last poem, 'A morning on Alp Lusgen', written in 1881 and revised in 1892, we find Tyndall reflecting on his beliefs and his place in the universe. The use of poetry to explore and express his inner feelings arcs across the whole of Tyndall's adult life. It gives us new insights into the man and into the social context within which he lived.

One poem, written in Marburg on the cusp of the 1850s as he was starting to envisage a scientific career, and probably just as he was engaging with difficult and complex experiments to explore the phenomenon of diamagnetism, is particularly revealing of the development of Tyndall's self-fashioning. The poem begins:

> The heights of Science woo me, and I clamber
> With patient strides the mountain's rugged back
> At times o'er flinty boulders slowly wending
> Beat by the storm while clouds obscure my track.[40]

This poem is a self-exhortation to the hard work and individual discipline needed to try the 'metal of his manhood' against the challenges facing him. It also speaks of the muscular professional science, a direct affront to the gentlemanly aristocratic science, that Tyndall came to personify, and promote in such books as *The Glaciers of the Alps* (1860) and *Hours of Exercise in the Alps* (1871), each of which consists of a part describing the author's alpine adventures followed by another devoted to his scientific investigations of the icy physical phenomena encountered there.[41] Nevertheless, poems like this, exploring his work ethic, his rejection of the constraints of society and his joy in a humble approach to great intellectual and scientific work, are the exception. The poem 'Society' and the fragment 'All smatterers are more brisk and pert',[42] both written at a similar time to 'The heights of Science',[43] are the only other clear examples of this.

Unlike the regular exhortations to personal discipline in his journals, most of the poems instead reveal a complementary side to Tyndall's character. Many are written purely to amuse his female friends or his network of male colleagues. It is in the remainder that the emotional content is most evident. Three are sensitive eulogies to the dead: to his father ('There is no cloud in heaven tonight'),[44] to a friend McArthur ('To McArthur'),[45] and to Dean Bernard ('On the death of Dean Bernard').[46] Others, such as 'Dont you remember love',[47] explore his intimate relationships with women, whether real or imagined, in heartfelt terms. Their introspection is not concerned with self-formation but with emotional self-reflection. Not all are just a young man's poems. 'To the moon',[48] probably written to his close (and married) friend Juliet Pollock, dates to 1863, when Tyndall was in his early 40s.

Tyndall's early verse is undistinguished, prone to archaism and clichés, such as 'zephyrs',[49] a 'vaulted sky' and women with 'Parian brow' and 'snowy breast'.[50] Beset by such drab poeticism and facile rhymes and sentiments, the early poetry has all the unguarded disclosures and unconscious betrayals that often make bad poetry a uniquely valuable resource for the historian of ideas and emotions. Tyndall describes such verse as 'Doggrel' and 'rubbish',[51] and, as was observed earlier, is not in the habit of calling himself a poet. Some of his jocular verses from the 1840s include a mocking first-person reference to 'this poets heart' ('Oh Mary pon my soul') and similarly to the bathos of an effort by his friend Ginty, as 'the poets fervour fled' in his 'chilly valentine' ('A desolate forlorn swain').[52] Another of Tyndall's poems, dating from 1849, when he was studying at Marburg, advertises its inadequacy to the extent of denying that it was written by a poet; 'I cannot write of love as poets do'.[53]

The humour is predominantly juvenile. 'A snail crawled forth' is revealing in its untrammelled dislike of 'This most repulsive snail | Leaving behind his filthy track'.[54] Tyndall shows no scientific interest in the snail's structure or motion, the fascinating laying out of its own road, but simply adolescent repugnance. There is heavy-handed humour in other pronouncements: 'With cloudy head', for example, was written about a flea, whereas 'On leaving Westmorland' is a practical joke on Ginty that caused considerable social embarrassment.[55] Tyndall is not averse to comic stereotyping offensive to the modern eye in 'An Hibernian's song. To—',[56] in which he satirises the Irish character.

In a further deprecatory reference to one of his early poems, Tyndall observes that 'The lines are worthless but they mark a tendency'.[57] He made this note twice, the first time probably in Marburg, the second very late in life, around 1891, allowing such propensities to be discerned more clearly in retrospect. The lines he is referring to in this poem express his abiding feelings for Nature:

Large has my love for Nature been,
    I loved her from a child
I loved her in her summer sheen
    And when the winter wild
Wrapped storms around her awful brow,
    And ocean formed a throne
To bear her, Queen and conqueror,
    My love was her's alone

Tyndall regards Nature as commanding, lifelong, loved in all her convolutions – a monarch exercising the highest power on his feelings. He uses the convention of addressing Nature as female. In 'The sea holds jubilee' he writes joyfully of 'the sympathetic land | Shaking her hazel tresses in her mirth'.[58] 'From the high hill' has 'courteous Nature in her haught abodes.'[59] In 'The day is gone',[60] 'weeping flowers', by the 'darkling stream', 'fringe its side', evoking the 'darkfringed eyes' which so beguile him in 'To Elizabeth'.[61] Beer notes in *Darwin's Plots* that this feminine identification of Nature follows a long tradition, from Ovid to Tyndall's contemporaries such as Charles Darwin and Gerard Manley Hopkins. She highlights two effects: to create a benign efficiency in the natural world and to distinguish Nature from God.[62] Tyndall harnesses a further aspect, the wildness of Nature: 'winter wild | Wrapped storms around her awful brow',[63] a trope he uses elsewhere. 'Dark clouds may gather, hostile thunder roll';[64] 'stark and grim upholding summits dreary';[65] 'o'er flinty boulders slowly wending | Beat by the storm while clouds obscure my track',[66] he writes of his struggle for scientific recognition. In addition, feminine Nature for Tyndall can be related to his own perceptions of and response to women: enchantingly beautiful, as challenging in her mountain fastness as an articulate or impertinent woman who speaks her mind, an overwhelming power on the senses. And in the Queenly stanza quoted, he has a unique example of the gender in mind. The lines culminate in the poet's oath of allegiance to an imperial majesty, 'Queen and conqueror', Britannic in her capacity to rule the waves, for whom the enthroning ocean is her apotheosis. His chivalric vow of a life of service to Nature is equally one to Queen and Country. The poem can accordingly be read in relation to the partisan political poems from the 1840s. It can be seen to corroborate the description that Sir William Harcourt applied to Tyndall in 1890 of being a 'scientific Orangeman'.[67]

The resemblance of Nature to Victoria that emerges in this short poem does not 'mark a tendency'. It is all the more telling for not having been one that he would have had consciously in mind. Rather it illustrates the enhanced capacity that poetry has to disclose, or betray, assumptions and attitudes belonging to the writer. Tyndall's brief commentary on the poem recognises this interpretative function, that it is upon reflection, especially with the benefit of hindsight, that incipient meanings and patterns become apparent in poetry, much as they may do for the scientist in nature. Written during the pivotal period of his life when he was studying at Marburg, and soon to become a man of science, Tyndall's poem takes stock of his abiding relationship to Nature. It yields a personal, fundamentally romantic, characterisation of Nature that Tyndall nevertheless brings to the materialist cosmology he developed and for which he became so notorious during the mid-Victorian period. The encompassing romantic unity and sublimity of the sea furnishes the grounding image for Nature in this poem. The *Sturm und Drang* of Nature's 'winter wild' yields to oceanic imagery, while her 'summer sheen' suggests sunlight playing on a calm sea and a smooth unity of vegetable and animal life, of shiny leaves, fur, scales and skin, uniformly reflective in the temperate season of their flourishing. The descriptive personification of Nature, with 'her awful brow', marks the tendency to romantic pantheism that becomes more overt in other poems, most notably 'A morning on Alp Lusgen'.

It is not only Nature that Tyndall characterises as female. In 'The day is gone', Tyndall expresses nostalgia for the landscape, as weeping flowers 'fringe its side' and 'fancy spreads her daring plume'.[68] Fancy is similarly gendered in 'On leaving Westmorland':

> Farewell ye dark summits, where fancy has wrought
> Her loveliest visions—ye temples of thought,[69]

Fancy is female, an emotional and unpredictable response to landscape. In addition landscape is a fount of scientific imagination, accessing 'temples of thought' through this feminised instrument. As for Beer's suggestion that the feminine pronoun characterises Nature as being distinct from God,[70] for Tyndall the reverse is true as he develops a pantheistic holism of life and Nature, described elsewhere in this essay.

For Tyndall, Nature is a sweeping pantheistic sublime, lifting the spirits and engaging the soul, an aesthetic sensibility swelling the emotionally responsive organ of human nature. And for Tyndall, that soul is female. In the jokey, jaunty poem 'On leaving Westmorland',[71] he describes the 'dark summits' and 'loveliest visions' where his 'soul in *her* essence exultingly soared'. In 'Society' he finds 'my soul | Has the society of those *she* loves'.[72] In 'Tyndall's Ossian' he declares of his soul 'with sympathy *she* swells'.[73] In 'The past' the soul has fed upon 'the lovely past' until it is 'Blent with *her* very essence' (emphasis added).[74] There are many examples.

In this female attribution he follows the convention of his time – the temporal core of a nineteenth century during which the gender polarity of soul was reversed. As Herbert Tucker states in his essay 'When the Soul Had Hips', 'the masculinization of the Enlightenment soul was a mistake, and so was the feminization of the Victorian soul'.[75] William Blake heads up *The Marriage of Heaven and Hell* (1793) with the statement that 'Man has no body distinct from his soul'[76] – a standard gender universal but still a masculine attribution. Blake proposed a 'radical identification of soul with body', a stance, Tucker writes, empowered by poetic imagery and its 'tendency to blow the cover off ideas'. 'The century's poets', he states, 'were its major imaginers of soul.'[77] In his dramatic monologue *Fra Lippo Lippi*, Robert Browning writes:

> Your business is to paint the souls of men—
> Man's soul, and it's a fire, smoke, ... no it's not ...
> Its vapour done up like a newborn babe—[78]

harnessing the Blakean metaphor for soul. There ensued during Blake's time a change from the masculine or neuter – 'his soul', 'it's a fire' – to a feminine soul. The two versions of Wordsworth's *Prelude* illustrate the change. As Tucker points out,[79] his 1805 version reads:

> The mind beneath such banners militant
> thinks not of spoils or trophies, nor of aught
> That may attest its prowess

while by 1850 we have:

> the soul
> Seeks for no trophies, struggles for no spoils
> That may attest her prowess.

So in those 50 years, Wordsworth turns from 'mind' to cognate 'soul', from the masculine 'banners militant' and neutral 'its prowess' to the clearly feminine 'her prowess', seeking nothing.

When Tyndall refers to the soul, and he does so 52 times, in 34 of his 76 poems, it is so often in response to Nature. He sees the emotive sensibility as a feminine one and a response by the soul to the beautiful and female world of Nature. Soul is female not only by convention but also by extension from the natural world by which she is fed.

In his poetry and prose, Tyndall extends the figuration of Nature and explores the nature of soul herself. Mackowiak points to a letter to Juliet Pollock in which he writes of 'That solemn unison which the soul experiences with nature, and which is a thing essentially different from the intellectual appreciation of her operations',[80] differentiating feelings and reason. Yet his writings some 30 years later on the use of imagination in science open with a description of his work in the mountains of the Alps, where he wrote these lectures, 'to spur up the emotions ... (and) nourish indirectly the intellect'.[81] This indirect connection does seem for Tyndall to link his scientific imagination, that picturing of connecting and causal phenomena beyond the physical measurements of science, with his emotional life. The freeing up of emotions by the sublimities of landscape, expressed or encouraged by composition of his poetry, appeared to release his imaginative intellect. The romanticism of his scientific writing in later years reflects its expression in poetry in his youth. Certainly his later scientific writing is often deeply poetic, as discussed in more detail below. Consider the passage from 'Scientific Use of the Imagination' where he describes the mode of action of 'sky-particles' on light: 'They fill the Alpine valleys, spreading like a delicate gauze in front of the slopes of pine. They sometimes so swathe the peaks with light as to abolish their definition. This year I have seen the Weisshorn thus dissolved in opalescent air.'[82]

Poets in the nineteenth century struggled with questions about the nature of the soul, its unity or duality,[83] its relation to subjectivity and selfhood, the relation of *pneuma* to material body.[84] By mid-nineteenth century, it was regarded as a truism that the soul was the territory of poetry while science dealt with the material. Tucker takes us to Coleridge's 'Phantom' (1805, published in 1834):

> She, she herself, and only she,
> Shone through her body visibly.[85]

As he states, these lines embody not the duality of soul and body but *psuche*, the inextricable fusion of soul with body, an 'indwelling principle within organised life'.[86] There occurs an echo of this stance in Tyndall's pantheistic writing, as in 'A morning on Alp Lusgen' in its later form:

> The long grass quivers in the morning air
> Without a sound: yet each particular blade
> Hymns its own song, had we but ears to hear.[87]

Poetry provides for Tyndall the mode to express thoughts freely in ways which would not, on first view, appear acceptable, or relevant, in his scientific writing. Tyndall's poetry suggests access to 'the temples of thought' through the emotional and aesthetic world, stimulating his scientific imagination and enabling his communication of the complexities of that thinking.

In 'Scientific Use of the Imagination' he expresses the hope that 'you will manfully and *womanfully* prolong your investigations of the ether' (emphasis added).[88] This may simply reflect the presence of women in the audience at such BAAS meetings. Or it may reference the multiple gendered aspects of investigation, Blake's 'radical identification of soul with body', the intellectual–emotional dichotomy and the Victorian commonplace of the soul as the seat of creativity.[89]

Tyndall reflects on the emotional dimension in his 1855 poem 'God bless thee Poet!',[90] yet another verse disavowal of himself as poet. By this time in his life Tyndall is secure in his identity as a man of science and is confident to address his higher feelings:

> Thou mak'st me feel
> A force beyond the force which science knows—
> A life beyond her life, whose mystic seeds
> Are songs, thy songs Oh! fragrant brother mine,
> Which cause the heart to blossom where they fall.[91]

Having realised his scientific vocation Tyndall clarifies his ideas about poetry and the role of the poet, to whom he allocates the romantic ideology he gained from his early reading and other acquaintance with the likes of Carlyle and Emerson. His figure of the man of science and the poet as fraternally related assumes not only difference but also deep affinity. Tyndall did write some poetry during his career as a physicist, but much less and much better than he did earlier in his life. This pattern suggests a correlation between the discipline and quality of his professional scientific work and that of the mature poetry, a hypothesis that would seem to be supported by the lyrical nature of his scientific prose, which ostensibly led the spirit world to award him the sobriquet 'Poet of Science', and indeed the artistry of the theatrical lecture demonstrations he described in much of these writings. The more exacting pitch of intellectual engagement required and developed by Tyndall's scientific work and writing appears in turn to have resulted in more considered and sophisticated poetry, culminating in 'A morning on Alp Lusgen', which is here published and discussed in the fullness of its extant drafts and versions.

Homosociality

Oh! there are thoughts beyond revealing,
  Which from their depths defy confession,
Oh! there's a tide—a tide of feeling,
  Which finds no floodgate in expression![92]

Some of the verses that Tyndall wrote during the 1840s, when he was in his 20s, were published in local newspapers, while many others were addressed to female friends or to the male friends with whom he worked on the Ordnance surveys. In 'To Ginty' he cheers a departed male friend and colleague,[93] while the 1842 poem 'To Chadwick' renders the camaraderie of the group, which both works and lives together, in the emotionally distancing language of mathematics, a comic application of the preoccupations and parlance of surveying to the surveyors:[94]

Among the things I mean to mention
It fairly claims the first attention.
Divide by 5 an even score
The quotient surely must be four.
This fits our numbers to a man
For Evans lately joined the clan
Who thrice a day with nimble feet
Do wend their way to Butler Street.[95]

This mathematical proof of the surveyors' homosociality maintains a modicum of emotional aloofness in its tribute to their unity and kinship. Later in the poem the group are drawn together through their appetites:

At dinner now behold the group
Breathing the fumes of gravy soup
Oh! for an angel's pen to trace
The varied twists of George's face
High in the air his mighty nose
Its pleasure rests in sundry blows.
Their ponderous jaws the others ply
A dog's delight in every eye.
Till stuffed with flesh or tired of bone
They yield the fight and dinner's done.
At dinner tis my lot to serve

My office is to cut and carve
The sweat drops on his dewy brow
Attest what Tyndall suffers now.
'A small bit John' says George & Bill
"The merest morsel" echoes Phil.
Thus do I waste my precious life
Oh! happy thou who hast a wife!
Is there no maiden in the land
To snatch <u>me</u> from this glutton band.
To loose those feelings packed and pent
Like clouds within my firmament
To chase the fog with radiant eyes
And bid the sun in glory rise.

The characterisation of the men as a pack of dogs is meant to be comic but is also congratulatory, galvanising the group through their appetites, earlier in the poem with an account of breakfast, now with one of the carnivores' dinner, and the satisfactions of the 'fight' and 'dog's delight'. Tyndall resents being placed in the feminised role of the servant here, a waste of a precious life that would be obviated by having a wife to do such things. At this concluding point of the poem the group of men are defined summarily as 'this glutton band', and Tyndall continues his appeal for a 'maiden' to rescue him from this pack, not as a server of food but also the emotive 'To loose those feelings packed and pent'. Such lines suggest the cognate canine appetite that, with the other attributes of fighting and meat-eating, helps account for the pervasive cultural identification of this domestic animal with masculinity. The imagery does not exclude emotional release but speaks overtly of physical pressure and relief, with its dense rain clouds and quibble on the rising sun in the final line, facilitated by 'radiant eyes', the female attribute that preoccupies the young Tyndall more than any other in the early poems,

the lovely spell
Which works in woman's eyes,[96]

and sexually charged:

—thine eyes, sweet girl, which once
Sent through the succulent fibres of my heart
Electric bliss,[97]

The vignette of George's nose gathers significance from this odd context. Dogs too are identified by prominent noses, snouts, as by 'ponderous jaws', and the 'dog's delight' belongs also to George's nose, 'Its pleasure rests in sundry blows', which regrettably anticipates the imagery of release at the close of the poem. Two poems from 1846 are devoted to the nose of another colleague, Jack Tidmarsh. The first of these, 'A snail crawled forth',[98] is illustrated with three drawings of the nose. Tidmarsh is represented synecdochally by his nose, which is here identified with a male snail. This imagery, together with that of the earlier 'To Chadwick',[99] suggests the formula for masculinity specified in 'Natural History', a well-known children's rhyme dating from the early nineteenth century: 'What are little boys made of, made of? | … | Snips and snails and puppy-dog tails.'[100] The assemblages of 's' and 'n' word sounds that compose 'nose' and 'snail' can be mediated by 'snout', which may be an aspect of the unconscious or semi-conscious logic impelling this poem; 'they mark a tendency' of formal nature. The resemblance of Tidmarsh's nose to the snail is suggested by the creature's 'nasty tail', although the poem locates it insistently in slime. The snail is 'a jelly race' typified by his 'filthy track' of slime, his attributes figured with other bodily excrescences, 'With malice like rheum in his eyes', and cognate imagery: 'envy fomenting like yeasty milk | Thro' his glutinous heart did run'.[101] The poem describes the snail's malicious plan to attack a carnation, which would take the form of hurling yet another bodily secretion at 'yonder proud and pitiful pink', a wilfully diminishing, de-flowering, act: 'I will climb your stalk and spit in your face | And sully your beauty—I will—'. 'Tidmarsh's nose' supplements this poem with a positivistic description of the offending organ, 'Dirty within and misshapen without', along with a taxonomy of men's noses, a nosology 'of many beaks & noses queer', and a further observation:[102]

A fellow sits opposite
    Has such a nose
That I cannot really go to bed
    Till I compose
A bit of poetry showing its horrible shape
For in truth it belongs to regular ape
It is long—but Oh! Lord it is of such bone
If you saw it you'd stare as if you'd trod on your own
It is short—when compared with its terrible length
In fact it must be a nose of no small beer strength

To stand all the blowings it gets with his wipe
And now I'll give over [a kiss] for the pipe

Much as throughout these early poems women's eyes are the focus of their sexual allure, men, principally some of Tyndall's closest friends at this time, are identified by their noses. The gross physicality of these nasal disquisitions perpetrates the neurotic masculine ploy of expressing affection through personal insult. Like the related doggy trope from 'To Chadwick', it also pays homage to his friends' masculinity as ugly, antithetical to the feminine prerogative and ideal of beauty, represented by the pink that the snail attacks and virile in its overdetermined, indeed hysterical, preoccupations with slime and other bodily secretions. The effect suggests displacement activities of the sort that J. G. Ballard entertains in *The Atrocity Exhibition*: 'Results confirm the probability of [US] Presidential figures being perceived primarily in genital terms: the face of L. B. Johnson is clearly genital in significant appearance—the nasal prepuce, scrotal jaw, etc.'[103] The focus upon men blowing their noses also suggests the sort of masculine exceptionalism that until quite recently impelled the marketing of specifically 'man-sized tissues'. Nose-blowing is prompted by women, symptomatic of masculine emotional distress, in several of Tyndall's poems, most luridly in 'No more dear Bill':

Ive seen him wrapped in Cupid's trance
Ive seen him shiver in the glance
Adown his woebestricken cheek
As oer his fate his bosom yearned
The mucous in his nostril churned
And ever and anon would slip
In yellow ropes adown his lip[104]

But there is sensitivity here too. 'Pour mon cher Jack' takes a more intimate turn; it is an affectionate farewell poem to a male friend: 'how I think on the nights we have nestled together!'[105] It is jokey and jaunty but also physical and tender. His 'Aerial phantazies of youth' is again written to Ginty, as a loss or parting poem wrought through male friendship yet including early forays into female love.[106] It is autobiographical, nostalgic and indicative of a rite of passage.

These early poems bear witness to the young Tyndall inducted into strong homosocial bonds and cultures, which he arguably brings to the later contexts of the X Club and other such groups. The poems' unselfconscious naturalism also suggests a prepossession of the later scientific work. So many of Tyndall's poems demonstrate a homosocial bonding focused upon various conceptions of women, while Nature is described in one poem as the faithful alternative to faithless women, and in a further, related, development in his private emotional life and conquests, 'The heights of Science'.[107] These are political and petty forms of solipsism that may bear a relation to the grand romantic solipsism of 'A morning on Alp Lusgen'.

Love and loss

Several of the poems are poignant with loss and parting: the male friendship poems; others to women such as 'Such bliss',[108] and the beautifully controlled 'The star that gems life's morning sky':

> Ah! No, t'is gone, t'is gone, and never
>   Mine such waking bliss can be;
> Oh, I would sleep, would sleep for ever,
>   Could I thus but dream of thee![109]

The poem 'We must part a while' stands out for its directness. It appears to be a final statement to whomsoever this lady is, or to himself to stiffen resolve. 'Fear not' he says – to whom, we know not – 'this is my last resolve, and this | My parting letter'. The only hint that this does involve the object of his feelings is the earlier line 'We must endure it'.[110]

Tyndall's writing of landscape is often concerned with memory of childhood days, as in 'Dont you remember love'.[111] Tyndall was permanently on a journey – physically from Ireland to Marburg and beyond via Preston and Queenwood, relocating with the seasons between the Alps and London, and eventually settling in Hindhead with his wife Louisa. He travelled socially and scientifically. The sense of past days infuses many of his poems.

Tyndall frequently uses eyes as a symbol of beauty and a metaphor for love, indeed for capture, where they are seen to exert powers of 'witchery'.[112] In 'To Chadwick' a wife is desired:

> Like clouds within my firmament
> To chase the fog with radiant eyes
> And bid the sun in glory rise.[113]

while 'Such bliss' is a charming love poem where the bliss 'lies | Hid within thy lovely eyes'.[114] 'Suggested on hearing High Mass in St Wilfred's Chapel' has:

> here the tears
> of pure pureness, fill the dark fringed eyes
> Of lovely penitents, while ghostly fears
> Sweep from their downy cheeks the vermeil dyes—
> The roseate tints which slumbered there—[115]

His landscape writing frequently acts as a metaphor for romantic love, as in 'Various Couplets':

> He is gone but behold
>   How the veils of the sky
> With their soft silver fringes
>   Roll silently by[116]

'Fringes' for Tyndall are equally likely to refer to landscape or to romantic glances, as in 'the dark fringed eyes | Of lovely penitents' and his poem 'To Elizabeth' where he asks 'do those darkfringed eyes still beam, | As lightly as they beamed on me'.[117] In 'Aerial phantazies of youth' Tyndall rejects the idea that the heavenly glow dwells in '"lovely Mary's" diamond eyes':

> Ah! no—it shines upon the breast
> Of every billow wild and high
> Which rears aloft its foamy crest,
> Rebellious to the darkened sky—
> ...
> There is a ray of magic power—
> A glorious sunbeam from the West!
> Which calls to life thy buried love—[118]

Landscape is intertwined with romantic love and allows emotions to be freely expressed. A sense of perturbance is evident: 'Oh! there are ideas which dart— | Like meteors thro' the midnight air'. Romantic emotion and fervour are inextricably bound with the varied character and seasons of the landscape – its wildness and gentleness. Both Mary Edwards and Ellen, possibly Ellen Wall from Kinsale of the 'raven plume', are joyfully woven into this poem.[119] The 'holy glow— | A beam' which '"gilds thy every song"!' resides in the crossing from 'New Babel' (Liverpool) to Kinsale, so this references also his pleasure in returning to Ireland.[120]

> Yes—there its nucleus dwells, to bless
> Thy morning thought—thy midnight sigh

yet:

> There clusters too 'the raven tress'
> There radiates the lustrous eye—

So in this youthful poem, love of home, of beautiful young women, of wild nature and the seas in all their moods and splendour are exuberantly comingled in an ecstatic celebration of youth, using the scientific language of light and matter – beams, nucleus, radiation, lustre, meteors – which continued to populate his poetry. He ends with a quote from Moore's 'Lalla Rookh' (though he mistakenly references it as Byron): 'oh! there are looks & tones which dart | An instant sunshine thro the heart'.

In so many of these poems, technical language is used for light and the mechanisms by which it falls on eyes, so in 'Acrostic (Jane)' we find 'E. ach dark beaming lay of thy beautiful eyes'.[121] Tyndall had a scientific fascination with light throughout his life. In the summer of 1844 he wrote a somewhat naïve letter to *Mechanics Magazine* concerning perceived shortcomings in Newton's particle theory of light.[122] He gave lectures on light at Queenwood School in 1851 and on many occasions at the Royal Institution, where he established a research programme that led to his explanation of why the sky is blue and to his discovery of chemical changes caused by light. Even before the development of his scientific career, scientific thinking and terminology infuse his poetic constructions. In 'Aerial phantazies of youth' (1843) he uses the term 'nucleus' to locate 'a holy glow— | A beam which "gilds thy every song"',[123] concluding that the source of joy or happiness is in wildness or wilderness. There 'radiates the lustrous eye' – a curious non sequitur, until one recognises his constant use of sparkling eyes to signal female attraction. In 'Acrostic (Miss Hebdon)', a simple and somewhat superficial form accommodates scientific terminology of dyes and ether.[124] A gorgeous opening line 'Morn smiles its loveliness on many a flower' extends to a botanic first stanza and a second which takes us out to the 'ether' of the boundless night sky. The much later 'To the moon' (1863) also resorts to scientific terms: 'Nor bromine richly brown, nor Chlorine green— | Not

Aqueous Vapour'.[125] His frequent use of scientific terms suggests that they are central to his cognitive vocabulary, that he is thinking already in scientific modes, seeing the world and his reaction to it through scientific frames of reference.

Most of his poetry predates his scientific research. In 1842, aged around 20 years, he writes in 'Acrostic (Christina Tidmarsh)', one of his earliest poems:

> R ays from memory's brilliant star
> llumine his pathway from afar

and

> I n thine eyes translucent light
> D eeply, darkly, purely, bright[126]

The 'rays' illumining, and the 'translucent' light, give romantic and emotional colour to phenomena he will spend later years investigating in the most systematic manner. He already appears as a romantic investigator of the natural world.

Tyndall writes often of the enchantment of ladies' eyes, yet with a strange relationship to light itself. So in 'From the high hill', 'The light of ladies' eyes shed ecstacy'.[127] In 'Beacon Hill', the

> belted legions …
> … stand in battle for those starry eyes
> To shield their bosoms pure from slight or wrong[128]

Putting aside the non sequitur – presumably it is the owners of the 'starry eyes' who need protecting – here the eyes are a synecdoche for beautiful womanhood. In 'Society', Tyndall writes of

> Beautiful Nature! boundless source of bliss,
> …
> With eyes more true than woman's, pouring light
> Over empyreal hills! My queen, my bride![129]

Nature and women are again Tyndall's sources of uplift or joy, yet here by 1847 he moves from unalloyed adoration of womanhood to the idea that Nature is constant but women fickle, a theme to which he returns. There is a developmental scale to Tyndall's writing on women, as he moves from adolescent adoration from afar, idealisation, to more nuanced and experienced readings of the opposite sex.

In 1848, on the death of his father, he pens 'Alone', finding solace in the 'solemn grandeur of the night,— | It is not joyless thus to be alone'.[130] Rather he condemns the over-literal or material perception of the natural world:

> The joylessness is his whose glossy eye
> Depicts eternals faithful as the lens,
> Whose iris can refract the slanting ray,
> And retina receive the landscape fair,
> And nothing more,—

So the emerging man of science gains spiritual solace from the landscape. As Beer notes, Tyndall was one of several scientists and novelists who 'were aware of the imaginative nature of their enterprise'.[131] His use of scientific terminology to describe the grandeur of the scene is therefore particularly notable, as is his use of some beautiful phrases – the 'mazy waltz', the frost-work 'evanescent as a dream' which melts in an infant's hand in this poem. Scientists of Tyndall's generation still shared a common language with other educated readers, rather than a hermetic discourse that excluded the well-read scientific layman. Scientific ideas of the time could be informed by literary ideas.[132] Tyndall's 'lapse' into obviously scientific jargon or language is however striking in 'Alone', and falls rather oddly on the reader's eye, as if he had stepped into a scientifically enclosed space:

> Nailed to the deep blue ceiling of the sky,
> My substitute for *gas*.
> …
> Sent through the succulent fibres of my heart
> *Electric* bliss, (emphasis added)[133]

Nevertheless, 'Alone' beautifully encapsulates the power of solitude and independence for Tyndall.

Women as disruptors

Tyndall's poetry charts a young man's exploration of the world of romance. At Goosnargh on 12 July 1843, he wrote three substantial poems.[134] In

'The aerial phantazies of youth' explored above, his romantic urgings take on great energy, a 'pulse of joy'.[135] The poem adopts a high tone, reflecting the immaturity of the title and the rapture of the content. Whence comes the 'holy glow' of exhilaration? Torn between a source in '"lovely Mary's" diamond eyes' and the wilderness, Tyndall chooses the latter.[136]

Yet this wildness touches his courtships too:

> My log should smoke and blaze and flame
> And consecrations from on high
> should sparkle round her sacred name![137]

This is also disturbing to rational thought: for Ellen he finds his

> swelling bosom's deep devotion
> Unutterable—while my mind
> Is crushed by mountains of emotion!

So early forays into the world of romance disrupt intellectual pursuits, just as Ginty is captured by Mary Edwards 'where Ginty's muse does gentler duty' but this 'wings his spirit quite away', transported but also captured by his feelings. Landscape is used as metaphor: 'thoughts of lovely Ellen raise | the murmurs of this melting stream'.

Women are often seen in these early poems as distant and unattainable love objects. In 'Such bliss', the bliss lies 'Hid within thy lovely eyes', inflected with a touch of the Orient: 'Eastern breezes softly sighing'.[138] In 'Acrostic (Miss Hebdon)', the love object combines both fair cheek and bright eyes, yet she is still a distanced and idealised figure.[139] We do not hear her voice.

It is notable that Tyndall was late to marry, in 1876 when he was in his mid-50s, and his bride Louisa Hamilton was about 25 years younger. Much of his conflicted feelings about romance and women, and his attitude to the state of marriage in potentially disrupting his scientific work, is evident already in his poems. Romance as an unattainable ideal is also seen as conflicting and disruptive to intellectual endeavour. From 'Alone' we see the context of his remembered attraction:

> ...—thine eyes, sweet girl, which once
> Sent through the succulent fibres of my heart
> Electric bliss, and served, perchance, to guide
> My footsteps for a time, wax pale and dim
> Amid the brightness of my present day![140]

The infantilisation of women, the 'sweet girl' seen time and again in his poetry, casts light not only on the age difference of some 25 years to his eventual younger bride but also his lifelong attitude to women's capabilities. He comments in his journal on a chance encounter in 1857 with 'A finely formed, handsome country girl': 'Thus it is that beauty without trouble to itself can confer benefit on men.'[141] In an undated piece he writes of women: 'I believe in their capacity to grasp and enjoy whatever the brain of man has achieved.'[142] While describing women as 'girls' is a conventional pejorative romantic trope which endures to this day, Tyndall's poetry amply evidences his positioning of woman as child, as a conveniently unattainable ideal to be utilised, and as a distraction from intellectual work. This was despite his later friendships to married women such as Juliet Pollock and the respect he held for his wife in his happy late marriage.

Though attracted to women, and expressing a wish to marry: 'Oh! happy thou who hast a wife!',[143] his romantic path was a rocky one. In 1858 he sought to propose to Mary Drummond. After a series of misunderstandings, it came to nought. In 1869 he wrote to propose to Mary Adair, but she gracefully turned him down and they remained friends. Both women were much younger than him.

The tender and controlled 'The star that gems life's morning sky',[144] still probably from the 1840s, is more personal. The charming first stanza of the title relies on an (imagined?) physicality:

> Thy head was on my shoulder leaning
>   Thy hand in mine was gently prest;
> Thine eyes so soft and full of meaning;
>   were bent on me and I was blest.

Yet still:

> No word was spoken, all was feeling.
>   The silent transport of the heart.
> The tear that o'er thy cheek was stealing
>   Told what words could ne'er impart.

The opportunities for misinterpretation seem legion; one feels the roots of the excruciating Drummond affair, where potentially tragic errors of romantic attribution concerning the young and desired Mary Drummond led to serious social embarrassment, with associated risks to the reputation of all concerned.[145] Yet still he writes conventionally of his romantic idyll:

When thou art near,
    The sweetest joys still sweeter seem,
The brightest hopes more bright appear,
    And life is all one happy dream,
When thou art near.[146]

He moves to an intimate physicality of 'Dont you remember love',[147] a carefully crafted love poem. The first stanza reads:

Dont you remember love, one happy night
You granted me a little crumb of bread
Slipped thro the mystic ring which circled bright
Your taper finger—underneath my head
I placed the precious fragment—then I slept
And Fancy, wafted to the land of dreams
Through bright arcades with zephyrs softly crept
Oh! listen—pencilled with supernal beams
Before my ravished eye the future brightly gleams

One can almost feel the fingertips which have rolled and shaped the crumb of bread, a tiny intimate talisman. The third line describes a ritual, slipping the crumb through 'the mystic ring which circled bright | your taper finger', clearly referring to marriage or betrothment, but to whom? The lady's identity remains unknown. Then he is alone, placing the crumb beneath his head and dreaming of the joys of courtship where 'the future brightly gleams'. He retreats to landscape metaphor as he ponders his lover's charms: a river or spirit 'gliding thro' the breast | of a signal vale', perhaps remembering boyhood times by the River Barrow. The stream is 'fringed' with shrubs like eyelashes. The landscape is melding into Tyndall's inner life, becoming one with it, a romantic blending of his emotional landscape in a church of the natural world. Indeed the lady's face becomes the land where 'chestnut leaves did quiver', a signal of emotional perturbation and of a romantic semiosis. Later, he states: 'It is not good for man to be alone'. Despite his reservations, he recognises that he needs a partner in life. He phrases this in religious terms as a transcendental imperative: 'Heaven's own dictum', and it is his own wish: 'Fancy thought so too'.

There follows a poetic catalogue of his lady's charms: 'And now I have disposed of many a grace', a controlling power base to deal with or throw away each dismembered part in this literary blason. His matrimonial intentions are out in the open and he is catching his breath with a formulaic if venerable form, from Petrarch to Edmund

Spenser's 'Epithalamion',[148] and satirised in William Shakespeare's 'Sonnet 130'. Tyndall uses tired vehicles: eyes are white, alarming as for a moment we see not dark beloved pupils but the rolled sclera of death. He commences an exploration of how to characterise the eye, a question he wants to pursue because of 'The depth of witchery which slumbers there'.[149] He searches for likeness in 'the star | That gems yon heaven—or in the midnight hue' or in 'archetypes' found in a 'glassy stream'. He is exploring the character of light and colour to capture their properties. We have dyes, hues, fringes, brilliants sparkling in a mine, and again the depth of witchery slumbering within. He labours on, then gives up. 'But why continue', he asks.

We are left with three sublime initial stanzas of astonishing intimacy. Tyndall must have been growing in sexual experience to write so intimately, even if much of what he writes is in the imagination. The concept of 'witchery' is noteworthy here. Coleridge in his 'Eolian Harp' writes of 'Such a soft floating witchery of sound | As twilight Elfins make', flowing from a harp 'by the desultory breeze caressed, | Like some coy maid half yielding to her lover'.[150] In later years Tyndall used this conceit in a sustained correspondence with his friend Juliet Pollock, writing in 1871 'now I shall halt in the midst of them to bless my friends, and among them Eolia'. He signs off: 'Yours ever, Boreas'.[151] Boreas is the Greek purple-winged god of the north wind; Juliet was Eolia.

Yet enchantment can also be captivation, a power of women which is uncomfortable or troubling to the ensnared male. In 'Yet, if to calm ungifted sight', he asks 'What may it be when spells of night | Are through the chamber spread?'[152] His 'Dont you remember love' continues in a version crossing the first text:

> Her eyes! Oh lovely Thirsa who can tell
> The depth of witchery, which slumbered in them there
> ...
> They murdered thro their fringes[153]

Charles Darwin, in his *Descent of Man*, proposed a dual mechanism of sexual selection among mammals, male aggression and female choice. Yet Darwin awarded the power of sexual selection in humans to males. As Russett points out, he asserted that men had 'gained the power of selection' because they were 'more powerful in body and mind' than women.[154] This is echoed by Richards, who describes his 'argument for the predominance of male choice in humans and the superiority of intellect and reason in men over intuition in women'.[155] The discomfort that Tyndall was feeling in female romantic power lies in the reversal of such ribald social and scientific assumptions.

In a humorous grotesque 'No more dear Bill', Tyndall declares his friend Ginty 'asped your whispers in the ear | of Sally—witching little dear'.[156] After this pejorative phrase he continues: 'the darling heard with many a blush | each overflowing tender gush'. 'Now boys', he continues,

> if me you ever find
> "Again by beauty rendered blind
> "or hung obeisant on the will
> "of woman—cod me then your fill

It is a revealing declaration, resisting the perceived disruption to their homosociality caused by women, their disconcerting romantic power:

> Thou good for nothing womans toy
> …
> like a donkey to a rod
> You bowed submissive to her nod

Her beauties are enumerated – her grace, her face, her eye, her brow. But, he says:

> what of this—should beauty bind
> In fetters an immortal mind
> Shall woman—creature of an hour
> Unnerve my soul and crush its bower

So women are seen as constrainers of higher thoughts and values, destroyers of the soul itself, destructive of a higher life. Lastly he adds the Kerry farmer:

> Who thus would crouch beneath the hand
> of woman and embrace her band
> which chains him to the trodden clod

This is vituperative beneath a humorous veneer. Woman is a threat to serious manly business, men's soul, the higher life. These are a young man's thoughts, but they are oddly resentful. There is a possible link to his marrying late. However, his attempts down the years to achieve matrimony point more to conflicting emotions on the subject and the pressures of his work.

Women and class

Tyndall's notions of class and social standing are conventional Victorian ones. The hymn 'All Things Bright and Beautiful', written in 1848 by Mrs Cecil Frances Alexander, wife of the Archbishop of Armagh and Protestant Primate of Ireland, sets these out: 'The rich man in his castle | the poor man at his gate | God made them high or lowly | and ordered their estate'.[157] In his poem 'Yet, if to calm ungifted sight', Tyndall resonates with both the hymn in its ballad rhythm and this social structure:

> The prince is in his pride again,
> The warrior in his mail:
> Stern puritan and priest are here,
> Gallant and gay, and maid as fair,[158]

One defence against the challenges of interacting with women is seen in the 'Ballad of the Isle of Wight' of 1 July 1856, by far the longest of Tyndall's poems.[159] An epic doggerel narrative poem, with overtones of other worldliness as well as comedy, it is nevertheless a detailed record of a day of rest and relaxation in the Victorian era. It clearly had fabulous significance in Tyndall's mind; a day of wonder, rejuvenation, indeed of scientific exploration, as his little party comb the rocks and sands of Alum Bay and take a frankly alarming sail home with a drunken skipper. In terms of Tyndall's attitudes to women, two themes are remarkable in this long text.

Firstly the figure of Mrs Wright is used as a stooge to Tyndall's adventures, a true 'Aunt Sally': the butt of his jokes, an immoveable buttress against which the wishes of the party can be thrown, despite her social position as a middle-class married woman. Male characters are far less prominent in his narrative, even though Richard Pears Wright, husband of Mrs Wright and a mathematics master from Queenwood, completed the party. As they trot out through the gate in a pony cart, Tyndall up front with Mrs Wright, he notes the 'mean mortar sphynx' who 'Turns her cracked buttocks from the morning sun'. We are clearly in for a roistering day. Mrs Wright cries 'But yes—see there is one!' as she spots a cloud marring the 'cobalt of the sky', leading to a eulogy by Tyndall on 'a thoughtful saint' who arranged 'angelic concerts' to 'warm his soul | With the dear memory of terrestrial joys'. Stirring stuff, as she helps stiffen their sinews – it is Mrs Wright who has:

caught courage. In her eye
Her husband read her soul—"we go" he cried—

as they scud away in their alarming craft. She is a cheerful person, as:

ever and anon a note of joy
Jumped like a singing thrustle from the throat
Of Mrs Wright.

However a touch of perceived gluttony follows:

Mrs Wright
Drew forth defiant from her wicker pouch
A crust, which she disposed of in a way
That proved she liked it;

She is clearly seen as greedy, 'defiant' even, in asserting her right to eat when she wished, though perhaps selfish in not sharing her morsel. She is a woman failing to act as provider to the masculine party, a threat to the perceived order, resulting in a vindictive little passage from Tyndall:

and were sickness there
The agitation of the inner deeps
Affinities reversed and fortunes turned
In wrong directions would have doubtless made
A different picture far of Mrs Wright.

She is a game lady, gathering seaweed in a dripping cave at Alum Bay, which puzzles some passing girls. Poor Mrs Wright has to 'claim' her own anatomy when declining a proffered arm from Tyndall while ascending a steep spur of the Down: 'For at each step she trod upon her gown | Which therefore needed lifting', she 'claimed the freedom of the arm'. She is well-turned out sartorially: when people 'thronged like pismires' (ants), a voice called out:

"Pray who's your hatter!" and the question spread
Like babbling echo, till a score of tongues
Thirsting for knowledge all enquired the same

Once more she is the butt of Tyndall's humour, an Aunt Sally or pantomime dame. They struggle with the long walk to Freshwater, and

'Poor Mrs Wright oft sighed | And wished us there'. She remains a figure of mockery, a

> poor soul quite spent
> With cheeks all suffering from the ungentle kiss
> Of scorching sunbeams oft and oft exclaimed
> "Oh what a journey for us back again".
> She thus forestalled an ill which never came:

Mrs Wright casts a shadow to the end in Tyndall's narrative. While Tyndall and Wright 'quaffed our ale', Mrs Wright was their 'only drawback' in that she 'Adhered to bread and butter, eschewed wine | And lemonade, and every other draught'. She is not one of the boys.

The second theme is the malevolence of local, working-class women, felt to be impertinent, brazen and thus threatening to Tyndall's enjoyment of this jolly day. So 'Two faces which seemed fair, and bright with smiles', on which the 'beauty of my heart confers a boon' emerge from behind a bush, to reveal 'two wenches coarse | Who grinned and nodded at me as I gazed'. He 'cursed their impudence'. The women are judged by appearance, objectified by the fact that they did not meet accepted standards of beauty and class. Tyndall could gaze freely as was his perceived right, but the frank and cheerful return of that gaze was seen as impudent: usurping and returning the masculine prerogative of the active objectifying gaze. He 'moodily' looks at the town clock, thoroughly put out by this encounter at 'half past nine' in the morning. Arriving at 'lovely Alum Bay' they explore a sea cave where Mrs Wright gathers up seaweed to examine it. Tyndall characterises the locals as uneducated or lacking in curiosity: 'Two maidens', one stooping and raising up a frond, 'exclaimed in accents coarse | "What can she want with rubbish such as this?"'

While noting a nasty passage about a 'lying' geology seller's deformity (he has a cataract in his eye) from which is inferred the 'cataract on his soul', locals in general seem antagonistic to Tyndall, or he to them. Either he misunderstands or he is standing on his dignity and suffers for it. Sighting a picnic group, he cries 'How capital' but, overhearing this exclamation,

> many a maiden with audacious lip
> Dipped deeper in roses, jeered me and my joy
> And asked me would I like to take a bit
> Yet manifestly meant me not to take
> Even if I liked it.

He is not socially at ease in this setting and resents the girls' comeliness while commenting on it. Or perhaps they are 'painted ladies' and again less respectable? – 'audacious lip | Dipped deeper in roses'. He thinks them impertinent and finds the encounter unsettling. Other working women he finds charming:

> A maiden [i.e. implying virtue] with a mild [i.e. unthreatening] voice and slender waist
> And darkling eyes from which a radiance gleamed
> Like Byron's lightning through the Alpine cloud
> Asked us upstairs

She conforms to Tyndall's expectations of modesty and grace. He speaks to her 'gently', telling her he has remembered her from the day before:

> It follows clear
> That the impression which you made on me
> Is deeper far alas! than mine on you.

She responds:

> The maiden bent her head and sweetly smiled
> And rose and lilly rippled o'er her cheek
> In waves of light while a more tender beam
> Broke from the crystal of her shaded eye.

Now comes Mrs Wright to this charming scene, disrupting a 'melodious current':

> Mrs Wright
> Damned the discourse by whispering she would tell
> My friends how I had "flirted" with the girl!

Tyndall is 'Stunned by the threat', yet:

> Drank the last light of her delicious eye
> And halted at the bottom just to sip
> The latest murmurs of her ruby lip.

On he goes, clearly visualising and objectifying 'Her image in my heart; her body where | The plane of the first lobby cuts the stair'. Images clash here: 'And now the hostler yields the whip and rein | To Wright, who tickles Fanny's ribs again'. This ambiguous scene flows on: 'A moment's hesitation—I am gone | And that dear maid may cogitate alone'. Here jealousy of simple working-class folk emerges:

> In the wrong place my jealous soul alarms
> Oh happy Bagman—Oh unhappy me
> The woe is mine—the waist remains to thee!

Again a woman has to actively retain her body part. As Sørensen describes it, in a pragmatic context humour is a powerful tool to 'challenge the prevailing order and transcend established power relations'.[160] It can be applied here to understand what Tyndall is doing in his characterisation of poor Mrs Wright and the young women of lower class who he feels are not acting in a 'womanly' fashion. Alternatively it can be argued that this is simply Tyndall at his most socially conservative, self-congratulatory, resenting the intrusion into his middle-class day by women: humour deployed in ways that are class-bound, neurotic and misogynist. Sørensen further comments that 'humour is not always carried out at the expense of those at the bottom of society, but can indeed kick upwards in order to aim for change of the status quo',[161] exactly what the young women were doing at Alum Bay. Young women who fulfil the required womanly norms and make no challenge cause no such response and can be romantically admired; the appearances and behaviours of others can be policed through caricature and ridicule.

At a different level in the class structure stands Juliet Pollock, an educated and accomplished woman of great charm and of a similar age to Tyndall. She was a talented water colourist, a published novelist, an expert on French drama and contemporary European literature and the author of a series of articles published in literary reviews. When Tyndall first met her, in the early 1850s, she was already married to Frederick Pollock, a manager at the Royal Institution and an eminent lawyer, who became a master of the Court of Exchequer and the Queen's Remembrancer. Tyndall developed a lifelong friendship with the family, including the three sons. His correspondence with Juliet over decades is extensive; they also met frequently. No hint of impropriety attends the relationship, yet it was close and intense. As far as we know, Tyndall only wrote five poems after 1860. One is the final 'A morning on Alp Lusgen' and a second a humorous limerick following his ascent of the Weisshorn. Two of the other three, and quite probably the third too, are written to Juliet Pollock. He also copied out and sent to her the 'Ballad of the Isle of Wight', a labour of no little time.

In June 1861, Tyndall composed 'The sea holds jubilee this sunny morn' (a draft dated the same day had 'The sea is joyful on this sunny morn'), written to Juliet.[162] It is a charming and tender sonnet in apology for missing a possible engagement with her and her family the following evening:

> Lady! my friend—thou surely wilt not frown,
> If lingering here I miss that other joy
> Of meeting thee and thine to-morrow night!

He is infused with contentment as he glories in the landscape of the Undercliff of the Isle of Wight:

> And I with heart content upon its verge
> Join in the laughter of the breaking waves.
> And glad, right glad the sympathetic land,
> Shaking her hazel tresses in her mirth
> While all her copses tremble into song

There is ebullience in the poem: 'copses tremble', waves laugh, foxgloves shake and roses blush. Brown's characterisation of such vibrancy as Carlylean 'romantic pansemiosis, in which all is radiant and expressive' applies here.[163] The poem utilises synaesthesia. There is evocative detail: the 'thickset trees' of the Undercliff, the 'scented woodbine', and it evokes not only the landscape but the warmth and tenderness, the maturity and contentment of his relationship with Juliet Pollock. The scene is admired 'not for sight alone, for beauty sends | Its finer essence down into the heart'. It is a metaphorically rich, mature love poem to a beautiful friend valued for far more than physical appearance.

Tyndall is striking in his use of landscape and the natural world to represent his joyful emotions as he escapes the pressures of work and society. His glorying in the landscape contrasts interestingly with its significance for a contemporary woman poet, Elizabeth Siddall. She is known as Dante Gabriel Rossetti's muse and often characterised by that relationship rather than as an artist and poet in her own right.[164] Siddall references the natural world copiously, but for her it signifies loss and death, often of a loved one.[165] So in 'It is not now a longing year' she laments:

> The river ever running down
> Between its grassy bed

The voices of a thousand birds
That clang above my head
Shall bring to me another dream
When this sad dream is dead[166]

The flat sorrow of Siddall's writing contrasts strikingly with the vibrancy and joy of Tyndall's, which sweeps together landscape, his emotions, his love for his friend in a holistic approach to the universe and his place in it. Mackowiak describes Tyndall's language 'with its breathless intimations of a quivering under-fabric to the structure of reality itself' and 'the hum and throb, the restless, rustling energy, of electromagnetic vibration that he overhears'. His writing gives great poetic energy and also captures his emerging understanding of the structure of matter and its underlying energies of 'oscillating atoms and molecules'.[167]

'The queenly moon' is undoubtedly written to Juliet, and it is likely that the more lengthy and intimate 'To the moon' is likewise. 'The queenly moon' is a compact quatrain:

The queenly moon commands the plastic sea
Which rolls around the world its silvered brine
And thus on Sunday evening drawn by thee
I'll roll from woodless 'woods' to 59[168]

It uses the metaphor of the natural world and the inevitable pull of the tides, to mirror the way in which he is inexorably drawn to 59 Montagu Square and Juliet. The woodless 'woods' are perhaps a play on his home in St John's Wood, as well as the glades under the sea. The use of the word 'plastic' implies his moulding by his friend, so by March 1863 he is still drawn to Juliet and influenced or formed by her. Brown points to the resonance with Shelley's rejoinder to Wordsworth in 'Mont Blanc': the 'everlasting universe of things' represented as a power that exists through consciousness as it 'flows through the mind, and rolls its rapid waves'.[169] Tyndall himself wrote in *Glaciers of the Alps*:

> Billows of air, in ever quicker succession, rolled over us with a long surging sound, rising and falling as crest succeeded trough and trough succeeded crest. And as the pulses of a vibrating body, when their succession is quick enough, blend to a continuous note, so these fitful gusts linked themselves finally to a storm which made its own wild music among the crags.[170]

Tyndall accesses the Romantic sublime through his scientific exploration of the Alps, paralleling waves in the air with those in the sea.[171] On a rare winter visit to Chamonix late in 1859, he forged his way towards Montanvert in deep snow: 'The Mer de Glace was quite glorious, … pure and white with its frozen billows steep, high, and sharply crested.'[172] The language of Tyndall's mountaineering exploits, his scientific experimentation and his romantic and emotional life are fused in these poems. As Mackowiak writes, Tyndall's own transport 'comes by *virtue* of thought, through his recognition of the interconnectedness of things, of the animating role of sun and tide-governing moon'.[173]

On Valentine's Day 1863, a date rich with its own significance, Tyndall penned 'To the moon', almost certainly to Juliet Pollock, and perhaps as a humorous piece. Nevertheless, it is a beautiful reflection on his affection for her, with the Hamlet reference drawn from Gertrude's speech: 'Let thine eye look like a friend of Denmark', 'Do not for ever with thy veiléd lids | Seek for the noble father in the dust'. In the first two stanzas Tyndall writes:

> Say does the crimson of the drooping rose
> When soft it falls upon delighted eyes
> Close up those eyes against the glorious sun
> Which gives all flowers their odours and their bloom?
>
> Or does the song of lark and nightingale
> Mingling at dawn along the Devon shore
> Make the full heart less fitted to enjoy
> The grander music of the gleaming sea?[174]

Tyndall asks here if the beauties of Nature interfere with appreciation of greater matters, 'The grander music of the gleaming sea'. He is not comparing the sacred with the profane. The lark's song is spiritual and evocative of finer emotions as it mingles with the dawn across the sea. He argues that his love for Juliet enhances rather than interferes with his wider love of science and the natural world:

> Is it not rather so, that where a love
> So large as that which fills my soul for thee
> Unlocks the doors, the smaller loves of earth
> Troop in without disturbance to the great?

The logic of the first two stanzas is reversed: the great love allows smaller matters to 'troop in' unimpeded.

As Mackowiak points out, the poem references Keats's 'Ode to the Nightingale':

> And haply the Queen-Moon is on her throne,
> Cluster'd around by all her starry Fays;

to a much more positive conclusion, 'remodelling' Keats's 'Adieu Adieu' into a tender moment, with a touch of humour reducing the intensity:[175]

> come nearer then my love,—
> Still nearer—stoop—a little lower—there!
> I kiss thy silver cheek, Goodnight! Goodnight!

He also seems to draw from Milton's hymn 'Let us with a gladsome mind', based on Psalm 136, with lines:

> Th' horned moon to shine by night;
> 'Mid her spangled sisters bright.[176]

Tyndall's poetry is bedded deep in Victorian culture, including the religious.

Later in the poem, there is a fascinating hint that he has been warned off: 'Dismiss thy fear; retract thy strong reproach | And bend thy beauty o'er me as of yore'. It seems as if Juliet has warned him that he is infatuated with the unattainable – she was of course married – and that Tyndall risks marring a deep friendship. He immediately evokes science, but tells her:

> Nor bromine richly brown, nor Chlorine green—
> Not Aqueous Vapour which the praying earth
> Swings from her censers underneath thy beams,
> Has ever caused my love to swerve from thee.

Juliet Pollock had advised him that he must not let infatuation interfere with his work, yet he argues that science would not interfere with his infatuation. Tyndall regards these earthly (scientific?) interludes as 'but melodies of minor note' which must have been doubly alarming for Juliet, reigning as his 'Queen of Stars', unattainable in the heavens, except that now he implores her 'come nearer then my love,— | Still nearer' until 'there! | I kiss thy silver cheek, Goodnight! Goodnight!'.

The previous lines where he attempts to reassure: 'Nor let thy lover for moment deem | The shock of worlds could move thy steadfast heart', are quite banished by the passionate envisioning of his love, the moon, moving ever closer to kiss the stars or himself. He follows in unfortunate phrasing: 'Thus nobly mated we shall love through time', 'and give the sinking hearts | Of men reliance on the force of love'. Whether humorous or not, Tyndall did have a reputation as a flirt.

By the 1870s, Tyndall and Juliet Pollock were exchanging further intimate letters under the pen names Boreas and Eolia respectively,[177] with the apparent knowledge of the whole Pollock family. It was perhaps Juliet's secure married state that freed them to be so open in their friendship and social intercourse.

Prose

Tyndall wrote little poetry after 1856. We know of just four poems that he wrote in the early 1860s. All but one of them, a limerick written on the Riffelberg above Zermatt after his climbing exploits, are associated with Juliet Pollock, as discussed previously. There appear to be no more until he wrote his swan-song 'A morning on Alp Lusgen' in 1881. Given the extent of Tyndall's papers in the archive at the Royal Institution, and the careful manner in which many of the handwritten poems were collected together (probably by his widow Louisa), it seems likely that he wrote few, if any, others.

What he did write in this period, as the drive to write poetry fell into abeyance, were extensive prose works. His first major book, *Glaciers of the Alps*, was written in 1859 and published in 1860, followed by *Mountaineering in 1861*, published in 1862. Though *Glaciers of the Alps* had both a scientific and a more general narrative section, Tyndall's first purely scientific popular book, *Heat Considered as a Mode of Motion*, appeared in 1863. The mid-1860s also saw the start of Tyndall's contributions to the major literary periodicals. 'The Constitution of the Universe' appeared in 1865 in *The Fortnightly Review*, to be followed by more than 40 others over the remainder of his life. In addition to those were shorter articles in places such as *The Reader*, *The Saturday Review* and *The Pall Mall Gazette*.

The narrative and writing style of Tyndall's books had a long gestation. Late in life, he revealed that Hugh Blair's *Lectures on Rhetoric and Belles Lettres*, published in 1783, had been influential during his early years in giving him what he described as a natural liking for good style.[178] This best-selling set of volumes would also have supported his desire for upward social mobility, an aim that, as Blair notes, an understanding of taste, language and style in refined literature would help to facilitate. Blair's passages on the 'sublime' in writing would doubtless have resonated with Tyndall when he was penning his later descriptions of glacier and mountain landscapes. Tyndall was well placed to appreciate and evaluate Blair's precepts on rhetoric and writing style and to develop the prose writing style and strategies that made his science books so popular with a wider public. Like so many at the time, he also practised and developed his prose – and poetry – by keeping an extensive private journal.

Tyndall's apprenticeship as a poet coincides with the start of his journals, during his early 20s. Indeed, many of his early poems are written directly into his journals. The youthful journal entries are mostly brief, and largely descriptive of events and people. Even so, lengthier narrative passages appear, including descriptions of a surveying visit to Mount Uniake in the Irish countryside, in 1841,[179] and to the Lancashire village of Goosnargh, scene of some romantic poetic compositions, in 1843.[180] It seems that he even started a novel, which he called 'a tale', in 1844 when he was back in Ireland after being dismissed from the English Ordnance Survey, though no trace of it has been found. Fanciful images that go beyond the requirements of factual record start appearing in his writing, as for example, at his lodging in Mount Uniake, Tyndall comments approvingly of his sheets, 'whose colour would rival Mont Blanc's whitest coat'.

As described before, several of Tyndall's early poems were published in newspapers under pseudonyms, generally 'Walter Snooks' or 'Wat Ripton', in *The Carlow Sentinel* and *The Preston Chronicle*. It was in these outlets that his first prose pieces also appeared in public, beginning with 'The German Student', a portrait of student life in Marburg, published in *The Preston Chronicle* in February 1849.[181] More followed in quick succession that year. The two descriptions of journeys he made, 'Excursion into Germany' and 'A Whitsuntide Ramble', are notable for their vivid imagery.[182] In the following extract from 'Excursion into Germany', Tyndall describes the impact of the rising sun:

> The grey dawn brightened, the sun climbed higher and higher, but was pertinaciously followed by a huge black cloud, which, like the Chinese dragon, seemed determined to devour him. Upward however he came, smashing his vapoury foe to atoms, and fixing his victorious glance upon the earth, seemed to ask, "Didn't I pitch into him?" The woods brightened up, the orchards bloomed with a

> fresher beauty; from copse and sky rolled streams of melody; bright clouds shook their silvery plumage over the hills, and flew away;—here the World Architect planted his compass, and, with a two mile radius, swept the river's bed, on one side spreading corn fields and meadows—on the other piling mountain ledges, covering the steep with beauty, and spreading at its feet the Weser, in which the woods might behold their own loveliness.

The rising sun is pitted against the huge black cloud, figured in an elemental battle of fire with water, of light against darkness. It is gloating rather than graceful in victory, a belligerent ball of fire: 'Didn't I pitch into him?' By vanquishing its foreign foe, the sun vouchsafes and enhances the earth beneath its victorious gaze. Later, Tyndall would emphasise repeatedly that it is the energy from the sun that sustains all life on earth. The passage renders all as active through its procession of verbs, but distinguishes two dynamics. While the earth is described as a romantic realm of Pythagorean harmonies, the overarching cosmology is thermodynamic in its clash of principles of heat and water, a meteorology that, like that visualised in paintings by J. M. W. Turner, suggests the physics of the steam engine (a subject on which Tyndall had lectured at Queenwood).[183] Tyndall's casually elaborated myth presents an odd proto-scientific collocation, with its hypotheses of design and atoms amongst its anthropomorphic sun and the Chinese dragon. It proffers a 'World Architect', depicted with his compass, like William Blake's rationalist figure of Urizen, and a black cloud that is construed imaginatively in the tapering form of a Chinese dragon and as composed of atoms, entities that at this time were still unseen and speculative, widely understood through their Lucretian provenance, teetering on the edge between ancient poetry and modern science.

The continuity between poetry and prose that this lyrical passage demonstrates is presented more forthrightly in his newspaper article 'A Whitsuntide Ramble', which contains within its narrative the poem 'Brave hills of Thuring',[184] the homage to Luther, that will be returned to later in this discussion.

In a series of five articles entitled 'Sisters of the Rhine', during November and December 1849, Tyndall produced an extensive narrative conversation on politics, philosophy and relationships, interspersed with rich descriptive passages of the landscape through which the Rhine passes and interlaced with occasional quotations from poetry.[185] Several more pieces appeared in 1850, a mixture of travelogues, incitements to others to self-advancement for his readers and early thoughts on the nature of scientific knowledge.[186] In 'Zig-Zag', Tyndall warns against attempts to ground theology in scientific knowledge: 'Science is valuable ... but we must beware of making it the foundation of moral or religious convictions.'[187] His views on the importance of the imagination and on the philosophy of science were emerging together with his mature prose writing style.

The most extensive examples of Tyndall's early prose occur in his journals, and particularly from 1856 onwards in connection with the landscape of the Alps. Many of his letters of the time, and both his early books that include mountaineering exploits – *Glaciers of the Alps* and *Mountaineering in 1861* – draw extensively on passages from his journals.

Shelley's remark that 'the popular division into prose and verse is inadmissible in accurate philosophy' is perhaps apposite here.[188] Tyndall's narrative prose was regarded by his contemporaries as poetic; 'his poetic prose writing is really wonderful', writes Henry Bence Jones to Emil du Bois-Reymond in 1869: 'I have been reading some of his letters to Mr Faraday from the Alps and it is quite wonderful how he poetises prose.'[189] Here is an extract from one of these letters, which dates from 1859:

> Bare, brown, and motionless the trees stood right and left, while the cliffs and precipices, mottled with the snow which clung to their ledges, took any form which the imagination chose to give them ... It was the silence of a churchyard; and the huge black pines which threw their gloom upon the road seemed like the hearse-plumes of a dead world.[190]

This passage finds in the Alps a similarly equivocal place for imaginative free play as Coleridge does in the Antarctic in his 'Rime of the Ancient Mariner' (1798), where snow, ice and mist invite expansive metaphysical reflections upon, and construals of, existence. While Victorian children's books are given to representing such frigid regions as fairy-lands of snow and ice, Tyndall finds in it an austere region which, rather than indulging the fancy, provides a match for the imagination in the plasticity and variety of its geological forms, 'the cliffs and precipices'. The silent churchyard is like the cursed ship, full of dead men, in Coleridge's poem, a bleak vision of existence through its end, its extinction. With the chiming 'gloom' and 'hearse-plumes' of 'the huge black pines' Tyndall achieves a strikingly desolate dystopian image, an emblem of entropic cosmological death. The power and originality of this image is distant from the poeticisms and cliché of his self-conscious early poetry, anxious to follow convention and to be credited as verse. The direct descriptions in the journal and letters free Tyndall from such bad faith Victorian versifying. They furnish a way forward for his poetry. Such imaginative exercises in the Alps culminate in 'A morning on Alp Lusgen'.

In his preface to the 1906 Everyman edition of Tyndall's *Glaciers of the Alps & Mountaineering in 1861*, John Lubbock, by then Lord Avebury, praised the 'vivid description and remarkable literary beauty' of his writing.[191] He quoted two long passages, but he might equally have had the following extract in mind:

> A multitude of mountains raised their crowns towards heaven, while above all rose the snow-white cone of the Ortler. Far into the valley the giant stretched his granite limbs, until they were hid from us by darkness. As this deepened, the heavens became more and more crowded with stars, which blazed like gems over the heads of the mountains. At times the silence was perfect, unbroken save by the crackling of the frozen snow beneath our own feet; while at other times a breeze would swoop down upon us, keen and hostile, scattering the snow from the roofs of the wooden galleries in frozen powder over us. Long after night had set in, a ghastly gleam rested upon the summit of the Ortler, while the peaks in front deepened to a dusky neutral tint, the more distant ones being lost in gloom.[192]

Tyndall's good friend Richard Dawes, Dean of Hereford, also found his writing poetic: 'You must not suppose that your Glaciers of the Alps have not been read by me; I got the book on its first coming out and I don't know that I ever read anything with greater interest or which gave me more pleasure, in fact you are both a philosopher and a poet, and I shall only make you too vain if I tell you the way in which I hear many of my friends speaking of Tyndall on Glaciers.'[193] So too did the mathematician James Joseph Sylvester, himself an accomplished poet and whose testimony is therefore perhaps more telling. He wrote of Tyndall as:

> a man in whom eloquence and philosophy seem to be inborn, whom Science and Poetry woo with an equal spell, and whose ideas have a faculty of arranging themselves in forms of order and beauty as spontaneously and unfailingly as those crystalline substances from which, in a striking passage of his [1868 Norwich] address, he drew so vivid and instructive an illustration'.[194]

It is Tyndall's writing about mountains that contains his most poetic prose. Starting with his explorations of glaciers in the late 1850s, Tyndall soon developed an intense relationship with the mountains.

His transcendental and pantheistic feelings found their resonances in the alpine landscape, shaped by his earlier reading of Carlyle and Emerson. He wrote in 1850, in a passage that expresses views to which he essentially adhered for the rest of his life:

> Emerson is a pantheist in the highest sense and so is Carlyle. I dropped an hour ago upon a very significant passage in the Sartor. "Is there no God then, but at best an absentee God sitting idle ever since the first Sabbath at the outside of his Universe and seeing it go?" At the 'outside' of his universe. I imagine Carlyle's untrue creed is folded in this Sentence. And here the difference between his faith and that of Paley's is very distinct. According to the latter God bears the same relation to the Universe that a clockmaker does to the clock. He is an omnipotent mechanic detached from his work. With Carlyle the universe is the blood and bones of Jehovah.[195]

The same sense of a holistic view of Nature was expressed in a letter of 19 August 1850 to Hirst, in which he wrote, quoting from Alexander Pope's 'An Essay on Man':

> I think the universe is best illustrated by a human body.
> All are but parts of one stupendous whole
> Whose body nature is and god the soul[196]

It was to such poets as Emerson that Tyndall turned to encapsulate his feelings. *Mountaineering in 1861* describes Tyndall's exploits during this year, which culminate in the first ascent of the Weisshorn. Each chapter is introduced with a poetic quotation. Of the 12 chapters, half are introduced by lines from Emerson's 'Monadnoc', which was inspired by Mount Monadnoc in New Hampshire. Others draw on Emerson's 'The World Soul', 'Ode to William H Channing' and 'Woodnotes II'. Three chapters draw on Tennyson: 'The Eagle', 'The Princess' and 'St Agnes' Eve'. The theme of each chapter is captured in its epigraph. For example, the epigraph to chapter 1 'London to Meyringen', where Tyndall's thoughts turn to his journey from the teeming metropolis to the Alps, is taken from Emerson's 'Monadnoc'. It expresses the need Tyndall felt, written often into his journals and letters, to escape to the Alps to preserve his mental equilibrium under the stresses of a London life:

> The mountain cheer, the frosty skies,
> Breed purer wits, inventive eyes;

And then the moral of the place
Hints summits of heroic grace.
Men in these crags a fastness find
To fight corruption of the mind,
The insanity of towns to stem,
With simpleness for stratagem.[197]

Other selections are equally evocative and pertinent.[198] Tyndall's shorter writings about mountains and the natural world contain similar poetic illustrations.[199]

Though *Mountaineering in 1861* is primarily an account of mountaineering exploits, Tyndall's scientific imagery is never far from the surface. In the very first paragraph, as Tyndall observes the Rhine from his window he conceptualises it through modern dynamics, a radical ontology of matter in motion: 'compressed bubbles snap like elastic springs, and shake the air into sonorous vibrations. Thus the rude mechanical motion of the river is converted into music.'[200] Similarly, 'Swiss life is poured like that of electricity in two directions across the bridge.'[201] Scientific understanding enhances Tyndall's wonder at Nature; it informs and facilitates his lyric appreciation of its phenomena. He expressed it in the following terms in his lecture at the British Association in 1867 to the working men of Dundee: 'It is the function of science, not as some think to divest this universe of its wonder and mystery, but, as in the case before us, to point out the wonder and mystery of common things.'[202] For such Romantics as Keats, writing here in 'Lamia', there was the danger of scientific knowledge depleting appreciation of Nature: 'Do not all charms fly | at the touch of cold philosophy?' Ruskin, in *The Eagle's Nest*, sought an integrated perspective on art and science,[203] but in a spat with Huxley and Tyndall in *Queen of the Air*, he sarcastically commented on Tyndall's explanation of why the sky is blue: 'So that the bright blue eyes of Athena, and the deep blue of her aegis, prove to be accurate mythic expression of natural phenomena which it is the uttermost triumph of recent science to have revealed.'[204] He implies that Tyndall's theory makes the wonder of the sky's blueness mechanical and prosaic. He did later offer what amounted almost to an apology.[205] It was of course no secret before Tyndall's discovery that the sky was blue, and Ruskin's comment merely serves to highlight the inadequacy of his efforts to fuse science with the mythology it supplants.

Mountaineering in 1861 is not entirely about mountaineering. It contains a short chapter entitled 'Reflections', in which Tyndall muses on natural law and the developing understanding of Nature that makes the concept of miracles, for him, untenable. He introduces the chapter with two lines from Emerson's 'Monadnoc': 'The world was made in order, | And the atoms march in tune'.[206] There is natural law, and necessity, but by implication of the reference to a musical tune, a creative principle behind it all.

Another reference to these lines of Emerson occurs in a very different context. As Gregory Tate has pointed out, Tyndall called on them again in his 1867 lecture on 'Matter and Force', after explaining the molecular processes underlying the transformation of liquid water into ice. Tate suggests that there are three ways of interpreting Tyndall's use of Emerson's language here: as mere embellishment; as supporting evidence for his argument (in that scientific knowledge and terminology 'has aesthetic significance, making the "music" of natural law and the "beauty" of natural processes more readily appreciable') or as 'epistemological and even (in a way that he deliberately leaves vague and undefined) theological or spiritual ... The "law" to which his atoms conform is not wholly distinct from the providential "order" that Emerson's poem identifies in the world's construction and operation.'[207]

In his final lecture on heat, in 1862, Tyndall declared: 'Presented rightly to the mind, the discoveries and generalizations of modern science constitute a poem more sublime than has ever yet been addressed to the intellect and imagination of man ... conceptions, which beggar those of Milton.'[208] Choi describes this as 'a new, secular literary form' and suggests that 'Scientific narrative, with its breadth of omniscient vision and its encompassing continuities, has come to surpass even the divine sweep of John Milton's narrative poetry'.[209]

Scientific prose holds a limited place in anthologies of nineteenth-century scientific literature, as Smith notes.[210] Compared to his peers and allies Darwin and Huxley, Tyndall is under-researched by literary scholars. Yet he deploys the literary tools of narrative, description and visualisation to enculturate his science and the manner of its communication. He is worthy of more substantial study, not only for the poeticism of his prose but also for the manner in which it draws on poetry.

The scientific imagination

Emerson became one of Tyndall's formative influences and helped to anchor his ideas about using the imagination to transcend experimental findings and look for the connections and explanations behind them.[211] Tyndall believed that the concept of the 'scientific imagination' is critical to the process of generating scientific knowledge and understanding, a position he expressed most clearly in his 1870 lecture 'Scientific Use of the Imagination' at the BAAS meeting in Liverpool.[212] The imagination brought an element of creativity into the process of scientific discovery, as Tyndall imagined and pictured entities that, though unseen, he believed would help explain the observations in the natural world. One might regard these as models, or even metaphors, but Tyndall saw them – atoms, molecules and the ether – even if they were 'imagined', as real entities. Yet he was aware that irrefutable evidence of their existence might be lacking, commenting with respect to the ether that 'although the phenomena occur *as if* the medium existed, the absolute demonstration of its existence is still wanting' (emphasis in original).[213]

Tyndall's article 'Goethe and Faust', published in *The Preston Chronicle* in 1849, is particularly revealing. He used it to express his early thoughts about the scientific and poetic imaginations 20 years before his famous 1870 lecture 'Scientific Use of the Imagination'. He wrote: 'In explaining many of the phenomena of nature we are obliged to use a sensible image as a satisfaction to the intellect; magnetism and electricity demands a hypothetical fluid; chemical combination demands the atomic hypothesis; polarization the hypothesis of ether particles and vibratory motion.' He went on to draw a parallel with moral nature: 'The moral experiences also have their imagery; and Goethe has given them under angels, devils, warlocks, and witches.'[214] But there is perhaps an asymmetry here. While Tyndall, as a scientific realist, believed in the independent existence of unseen or unimaged (at least in the nineteenth century) atoms and molecules, it is unlikely that he believed in the existence of angels, devils, warlocks and witches, except as human mental constructs. Indeed such entities belong to the realm of mythology, a category that Tyndall and many of his peers saw as including Christianity, accounts describing the phenomena of physical nature that modern science sought to banish and supersede. The poetic imagination begins with human consciousness and moves outwards to speculate upon its relation to the object world. Much as in Descartes, consciousness also provides an anchoring point for the possibility of knowledge for the Romantics. For such first-generation Romantics as Coleridge and Wordsworth, our subjectivity can gain knowledge of the object world not only reflexively, as the complementary principle by which we distinguish our selfhood, but also imaginatively as continuous with the object world, allowing us to see past appearances and see into the nature of things themselves. This conviction depends upon a post-Kantian idealist conviction that human consciousness and the object world are continuous, manifestations of the one principle, 'the one life within us and abroad', as Coleridge puts it in 'The Eolian Harp', ultimately the *logos* or God, the Creator. Without such undergirding structures of metaphysical idealism, it becomes difficult to distinguish the imagination from the frivolous function of the fancy, by which we can picture such things as chimera – it is merely speculative, hallucinatory, not an epistemological principle. Tyndall was familiar with such expansive romantic principles of consciousness and poetic imagination, which found scientific applications in the work of Humphry Davy, Thomas Beddoes and others, but needed to look at this relation anew and somehow to reconcile it to his positivism and his materialist science.

Tyndall recognised that the subjective nature of consciousness seemed inaccessible to, and irreconcilable with, the exploration and explanation of Nature as object, even though he believed that it must arise out of physical processes. Tyndall had read Kant extensively and would have been aware of Kant's account of the problem of knowledge that distinguished noumena (the thing-in-itself, inaccessible to us) and phenomena (which we are able to access empirically). Tyndall's recognition of the problem went back many years. In 1855, in a ramble across northern France, he mused: 'the man in this world, as well as the taking down of the structure after death, are certainly the work of molecular forces ... but how do thought and consciousness spring from these molecular combinations? ... Experience shows them to be twin phenomena, but is the association necessary? Can conscious thought exist apart from matter or can it not?'[215] In an extended passage in his 1868 Presidential Address to the Mathematical and Physical Section of the BAAS in Norwich, he went further:

> I can hardly imagine there exists a profound scientific thinker ... unwilling to admit the extreme probability of the hypothesis, that for every fact of consciousness, whether in the domain of sense, of thought, or emotion, a certain definite molecular condition is set up in the brain; who does not hold this relation of physics to consciousness to be invariable, so that, given the state of the brain, the corresponding thought or feeling might be inferred; or given the thought or feeling, the corresponding state of the brain might be inferred.[216]

But how? Tyndall believed that 'the passage from the physics of the brain to the corresponding facts of consciousness is unthinkable'. Even if we knew that motion in the brain is in one direction when we love and that it is in another direction when we hate, 'the "WHY" would remain as unanswerable as before'.[217] Materialism could not provide the answer, and indeed an explanation of this 'hard problem' of consciousness remains, to general satisfaction, unanswered still. Tyndall continued: 'Meanwhile the mystery is not without its uses. It certainly may be made a power in the human soul; but it is a power which has feeling, not knowledge, for its base.'[218] This is where Tyndall thought that poetry would ultimately play a major role. He regards poetry as more than some sort of mystificatory 'overflow' or valve to release the complexities or questions that disturb the reductionist and determinist schema of 'scientific materialism'. Instead, Tyndall is saying that there are some questions that cannot be answered and some emergent phenomena that cannot be explained and understood, with meaning, by reductionist and materialist approaches. He looks to poetry as the means of acknowledging and considering such transcendent questions.

Frederick Pollock drew clear parallels between the scientific and poetic imaginations in his introduction to William Kingdon Clifford's *Lectures and Essays*: 'It is an open secret to the few who know it, but a mystery and a stumbling-block to the many, that Science and Poetry are own sisters; inasmuch as that in those branches of scientific enquiry which are most abstract, most formal, and most remote from the grasp of the ordinary sensible imagination, a higher power of imagination akin to the creative insight of the poet is most needed and most fruitful of lasting work.'[219] In 'Cosmic Emotions', Clifford wrote: 'For the true poetry is that which expresses our feelings, and not my feelings only—that which appeals to the universal in the heart of each one of us. So it has come about that the world of the poet, the world in its emotional aspect, always lags a little behind the world of science ... We always know a little more than our imaginations have thoroughly pictured.'[220]

Nature, in Tyndall's worldview, is gendered and female, the object of the researches of the man of science. Male poetry is often addressed to the female object of desire, and Tyndall explicitly linked these in a letter to Juliet Pollock: 'But it is equally true in science as in poetry that "Nature never did betray the heart that loved her," and though the precise object at which the investigator aims may not be attained—may indeed be unattainable, still if he be only faithful to his task he is sure to be rewarded according to the method of Nature herself.'[221]

Herbert Spencer saw science itself as poetic, writing: 'Let us not overlook the further great fact, that not only does science underlie sculpture, painting, music, poetry, but that science is itself poetic ... Those engaged in scientific researches constantly show us that they realize not less vividly, but more vividly, than others, the poetry of their subjects.'[222]

The scientific imagination could only take Tyndall so far. Beyond it was the 'mystery' of cosmic purpose and meaning that eluded methodological materialism and was the province of the religious sensibility. A fierce opponent of religious dogma, expressed most clearly in the Belfast Address, Tyndall nevertheless recognised the human need for insight beyond scientific understanding, into what he would describe as the emotional realm. Here, he believed lay the true potential value and place of poetry, once frail human reliance on religious dogma fell away. Writing to an unknown correspondent two years after the Belfast Address he expressed it this way: 'Few I imagine entertain a higher idea than I do as to the part which poetry is to play in the future of this world. It will, I believe, have to take into its sole charge the feelings and aspirations which have hitherto found expression in the religions of the world.'[223] Probably some years later, in an undated letter that may be to the philosopher, pioneering semiotician and scientist Lady Victoria Welby, he wrote:

> [What] I want to [preserve] to humanity is the motive force which has been hitherto derived from religion; and the action of which it appears to me you do not sufficiently take into account. I want in short to preserve the ideal or poetic side; for humanity will never consent to the withdrawal of religion without some substitution of this kind. We must take man as he is and as he is he will never rest satisfied with the purely logical—He will demand the warming of his feelings as well as the enlightenment of his understanding.[224]

Tyndall expanded on this idea in his lecture and article on Goethe's 'Farbenlehre' in 1880. Though critical of Goethe's romantic science he nevertheless recognised his debt to Goethe as a poet and set out clearly the domains of the poet and the man of science:

> The emotions of man are older than his understanding, and the poet who brightens, purifies, and exalts these emotions may claim a position in the world at least as high and as well assured as that of the man of science … There is no fear that the man of science can ever destroy the glories of the lilies of the field; there is no hope that the poet can ever successfully contend against our right to examine, in accordance with scientific method, the agent to which the lily

owes its glory ... Nature embraces them both, and man, when he is complete, will exhibit as large a toleration.[225]

Though some of his contemporaries tried to tar Tyndall, the methodological materialist, with an atheist brush, he was no atheist and he had a keen appreciation of the religious sense. While few of his poems deal explicitly with religion, one that stands out, given the manner in which he later used it, is 'Brave hills of Thuring'. Written in Luther's Wartburg, inspired by his visit there, it celebrates the founder of Protestantism:

And once, when leaning o'er this ancient table,
As midnight clothed the world in robes of sable,
His candle waned—a shudder curdled o'er him,
When lo! the Prince of Darkness stood before him.
A moment's fear,—'tis gone—and Heaven-reliant
He lowered upon the fiend a brow defiant:—
"Or com'st thou, by permission, here to try me,
Or deputy from hell to terrify me;
The effort's vain—I fear thee not—I'll face thee,
And as an earnest, Oh, thou son of Evil!
Take that."—He shied his inkstand at the devil![226]

The poem was written in 1849 and published in a piece entitled 'A Whitsuntide Ramble' in *The Preston Chronicle*. More than 20 years later, at a time when Tyndall and his Metropolitan 'scientific naturalist' friends were in conflict with the 'North British' group of Scottish Presbyterian physicists, Tyndall sent a version of this poem to Maxwell. We do not know why, and no response from Maxwell is known, but we can speculate that Tyndall wished to try to make it clear that he was not the atheistic materialist supposed by some. He was, though, decidedly anti-Catholic throughout his life, as 'Suggested on hearing High Mass in St Wilfred's Chapel' attests:

The frown of Rome—like barbs and bolts it flies,
Piercing the soul, and crushing all its powers—
Before her mystic shrines th' immortal essence cowers![227]

In his response to criticism of the Belfast Address in 1874, 'Rev. James Martineau and the Belfast Address', Tyndall explained his frequent resort to the poetry of Emerson: 'The reader of my small contributions to the literature which deals with the overlapping margins of Science and Theology, will have noticed how frequently I quote Mr Emerson. I do so mainly because in him we have a poet and a profoundly religious man, who is really and entirely undaunted by the discoveries of Science, past, present, or prospective. In his case, Poetry, with the joy of a bacchanal, takes her graver brother Science by the hand and cheers him with immortal laughter.'[228]

For many in the nineteenth century, starting with Wordsworth, the Romantic most read by the Victorians, poetry was defined in opposition to scientific practice: the 'ideal' in opposition to the 'real', or the subjective and personally meaningful in opposition to the objective, dry and factual.[229] For Tyndall they were complementary, manifestations of different kinds of knowledge, as expressed by Wordsworth in his preface to *Lyrical Ballads*, but not opposites. Poetry, in a manner that resonated with Emerson, is described by Wordsworth in the 'Preface' to the *Lyrical Ballads* as 'the impassioned expression which is in the countenance of all science'.[230] Perhaps drawing on Wordsworth, though copied into his journal in 1855 after he had written it 'in a blank scrap of Tennyson's Maud', is Tyndall's 'God bless thee Poet!'. It ends:

> God bless thee! let me hear thee oft—Oh! come,
> When the cold brain o'erbalances the soul,
> When intellect untinctured by a hue
> Of feeling deems all Nature a machine,
> And life itself the product of a force
> Which acts it knows not why,—Thou mak'st me feel
> A force beyond the force which science knows—
> A life beyond her life, whose mystic seeds
> Are songs, thy songs Oh! fragrant brother mine,
> Which cause the heart to blossom where they fall.[231]

Scientific communication

Tyndall made frequent use of quotes from poetry in ways that helped communicate and validate his ideas at the interfaces of science, religion and human action in the world. For example, he quoted from Tennyson's 'Lucretius' in the Belfast Address and gave prominence to Wordsworth's 'Tintern Abbey' in some subsequent published versions of it. Not only did these resonate in terms of their content – 'Lucretius' immediately calling to mind the *De rerum natura*, Lucretius's long epicurean didactic poem, claimed for scientific naturalism by Tyndall, Huxley and others,[232] and 'Tintern Abbey' nevertheless evoking a sense of spirituality – but also the reference to such revered poets lent cultural credibility to his utterances.[233] He was not averse to using the suggestions of others. Following his lecture on 'Scientific Use of the Imagination' in 1870, there was a lively response in the newspapers. Tyndall had expressed the view that we should look at matter, as Goethe had, as 'the living garment of God', not as 'brute', reflecting his holistic and transcendental vision of matter, Nature and the universe.[234] *The Spectator* took this up, and suggested Goethe's lines from 'Gott und Welt':

> Was wär' ein Gott der nur von aussen stiesse
> Im Kreis das All am Finger laufen liesse!
> Ihm ziemt's, die Welt im Innerern zu bewegen,
> Natur in Sich, Sich in Natur zu hegen.[235]

The meaning in these lines echo those from Pope's 'An Essay on Man', quoted above, asserting that God does not stand outside Nature but dwells within.

But Tyndall had more to extract from Pope's lines from 'An Essay on Man' that he quoted in his 1850 letter to Hirst: 'All are but parts of one stupendous whole | Whose body nature is and god the soul'. In 1872, two years after 'Scientific Use of the Imagination' and two years before the Belfast Address, he used the lines to make a particular point about the knowledge of the universe vouchsafed by science, and the limits of science. Introducing his Friday Evening Discourse at the Royal Institution 'On the Identity of Light and Radiant Heat', itself an example of the interconnectedness of the natural world through the energy principle, he started the lecture as follows: 'Whether we regard its achievements in the past, or its promise and tendency in the future, all that we know of physical science … tends to confirm the dictum of the poet regarding the universe:—

> "All are but parts of one stupendous whole
> Whose body nature is"'

Here he stopped, omitting the phrase 'and god the soul', not, he declared, 'because physical science has arrived at any conclusion hostile to that clause … but simply because what the poet goes on to affirm lies outside the sphere of science'.[236] Tyndall uses here the meaning of the poetry, with its conservative cultural authority and canonical aura, to buttress and validate his argument.

He did the same in many of his notable speeches and writings. Tyndall published more than 40 articles in the major literary periodicals. About half of these were published, with other items including lectures and speeches, in his books *Fragments of Science* (editions from 1871) and *New Fragments* (1892). Taken together, they cover scientific topics, the relationships between scientific and religious outlooks, and broader observations of the natural world, including the Alps. Again, he uses poetry to enhance the impact of his words in several of these pieces, and particularly in more controversial areas. For example, an 1880 lecture on the contentious issue of 'The Sabbath' ends with resounding and motivational quotes from Thomas Hood's 'Ode to Rae Wilson'.[237] Likewise, his presidential address to the Birmingham and Midland Institute in 1877, 'Science and Man', quotes from Tennyson's 'Ænone' to illustrate the sentiment of duty and from Emerson's 'The Higher Life' to support his argument that the religious sense is derived from man's moral nature, not the reverse.[238]

During his life, Tyndall wrote three major books on scientific ideas and discoveries designed for a popular audience: *Heat Considered as a Mode of Motion* (1863), *Sound: A Course of Eight Lectures Delivered at the Royal Institution of Great Britain* (1867), and *Six Lectures on Light: Delivered in America in 1872–1873* (1873), although to these could be added part of his *Glaciers of the Alps* (1860) and *The Forms of Water in Clouds and Rivers, Ice and Glaciers* (1872). Yet unlike the case with his writing in *Mountaineering in 1861*, Tyndall made limited reference to poetry in these books. The same is true for the purely scientific articles he wrote for the literary periodicals. It is as though the science stood for itself and needed no further validation or illustration. The few interpolations of poetry are almost incidental. There is just one in *Heat Considered as a Mode of Motion*, when Tyndall resorts to Shakespeare's *Twelfth Night* when describing the ability of odorous chemicals to absorb heat:

> The sweet south
> That breathes upon a bank of violets,
> Stealing and giving odour,[239]

Sound contains no references, and *Six Lectures on Light* only two. In the first he quotes Tennyson, to offer a vivid image, as he makes a point about the identity of colour of incident and reflected light:

> The moon appears to us as if
> 'Clothed in white samite, mystic, beautiful;'

but were she covered with the blackest velvet she would still hang in the heavens as a white orb, shining upon our world substantially as she does now.[240]

In the second he draws on Emerson, to capture a sense of the exquisite effects produced by wave motion:

'Thou can'st not wave thy staff in the air
Or dip thy paddle in the lake,
But it carves the brow of beauty there,
And the ripples in rhymes the oars forsake.'[241]

'A morning on Alp Lusgen'

Tyndall's final poem, 'A morning on Alp Lusgen',[242] stands apart from his earlier work. Not only is it the most powerful and significant piece that he wrote, but it comes after a poetic silence of almost 20 years. It is as though Tyndall's pioneering work as a public-facing science communicator, in his prose writings and in his theatrical lecture demonstrations at the Royal Institution (from 1853 to 1887) and the versions of them he published, required him to hone his lyrical and rhetorical powers of expression, so that he effectively emerges as a new poet when he returns to writing poetry again in the 1880s.

'A morning on Alp Lusgen' is the most studied of Tyndall's poems,[243] but some salient points have been missed. O'Gorman gives the publication as 1892,[244] as the last piece in Tyndall's final book *New Fragments*,[245] while noting the existence of undated drafts. Mackowiak states that it was drafted c.1890,[246] while Brown earlier suggested c.1878.[247] It has not generally been noticed that a version of the poem was first published under the title 'From the Alps: a fragment', signed 'J. T.', in *The Pall Mall Gazette* of 16 August 1881. Contemporaries may have guessed the authorship, but there is only one reference in Tyndall's extant correspondence to this publication. Tyndall wrote to his close friend Hirst on 9 August 1881 to tell him, self-deprecatingly, of its forthcoming appearance: 'I purposed sending you a poem, but instead of that sent a rigmarole to the Pall Mall Gazette.'[248] It is no rigmarole. Reading the poem, it is easy to imagine that it was written not just from but in the Alps, from Tyndall's perch on Alp Lusgen, looking far below to the checkerboard valley and the Rhône and across to the distant mountains on the Italian border. It has that powerful sense of place.

The poem is constructed in two parts, as O'Gorman has pointed out.[249] The first part expresses Tyndall's sense of the beauty and mystery of the world, its transcendental nature and our inability to fathom how it might have come into being. Brown has previously described the poem's debt to the chapter on 'Natural Supernaturalism' in Carlyle's *Sartor Resartus*, which Tyndall first read in 1850: 'His "excess of light" can be matched with Carlyle's image of luminous superabundance, "Light-sea of celestial wonder," and his trembling grass compared to "every grass blade," through which the glory of a present God still beams.'[250] As Mackowiak noted, its scene-setting echoes Wordsworth's 'Tintern Abbey', which Tyndall had quoted to provide the context for the Belfast Address some seven years earlier.[251] Tyndall calls to mind both the peaks and valley laid out to view and the pines, gentians, whortleberries, marigolds and Alpine roses that can still be seen in profusion up on Bel Alp. Colour suffuses the poem: the orient crimson; the azure gentian and sky; the freshest green vale; the purple berries and azaleas; and the yellow marigolds. The beauty is simply there. It was not created for the benefit of humankind, a belief Tyndall explicitly expressed elsewhere.[252] The meaning of the poem is shot through with resonances of Wordsworth, Carlyle and Emerson, and an almost religious worship of the natural world. Emma Mason, in her chapter 'Emotion, Feeling, Affect', remarks that 'James Martineau's proclamation that "worship is an attitude which our nature assumes, not *for a purpose*, but *from an emotion*" [Martineau's emphasis] typifies the connections between feeling and religion',[253] which is a connection that Tyndall himself recognised.

The second part is a tribute to Carlyle, such a strong early influence, with Emerson, on Tyndall's thought and action. Tyndall echoes Carlyle's repudiation of religious dogma, represented in the poem by the arch-Catholic 'Jesuit oriflamme', and Carlyle's demand for the 'Might' of strong leaders to be based on 'Right' if they were to act morally and to be worthy of respect and following. Tyndall here invokes Napoleon as anti-hero, whose deeds have vanished 'evanescent'. The homage to Carlylean thought that the poem represents is surely a response to the death, six months earlier on 5 February 1881, of Carlyle himself, Tyndall's hero and friend. The poem reads as though written on Alp Lusgen in that summer of 1881, through the intensity of Tyndall's memory of his friend and of the landscape in which he was embedded.

As argued earlier, we can reasonably assume that Tyndall's apparent poetic silence, from the early 1860s to the early 1880s, is a genuine one. There is no evidence, from his journals, letters or notes, that he wrote other poetry during this period. A combination of causes may explain this hiatus. Most obvious is the sheer pressure of Tyndall's work. From around 1860 onwards, as his increasing public profile drew him evermore into the distracting, hectic swirl of soirées and dinner parties, his commitments to both research and lecturing were piled on top. Tyndall had made his crucial discovery of the absorption of radiant heat by gases in 1859, and a huge research programme stood ahead of him. At the same time, perhaps partly driven by financial insecurity, he had added to his existing lecturing and examining responsibilities the demands of the professorship of physics at the Royal School of Mines, with its requirement to give an extensive series of examined lectures each year. He may not have been writing poetry, but he was certainly writing. He had just finished *Glaciers of the Alps*, his first book, and had started writing his popular book *Heat Considered as a Mode of Motion*, published in 1863. Articles in *The Reader* and *The Saturday Review* in the early 1860s would soon be followed by regular contributions to the literary periodicals, starting with 'The Constitution of the Universe' in *The Fortnightly Review*.[254]

The development of Tyndall's prose writing may also help explain the lack of poetry. The prose writing itself, especially in relation to mountains, landscape and the feelings they evoke, became an outlet for Tyndall's emotions and for his ideas about the nature of the universe. His long apprenticeship, both in reading and writing poetry, spilled over into the prose writing that, as we have seen, was widely regarded as poetic. Only after two decades did he return to poetry, and then only for one instantiation. He had learnt much in the interim. Gone are the overblown phrases and over-dramatic images. This poem is a mature statement, infused with the narrative style that he had now developed.

'A morning on Alp Lusgen' might seem to blaze suddenly like a meteor after 20 years. But it has a deep history that brings Tyndall's transcendentalism and pantheism into harmony with his materialism. It is no surprise that the poem was written on Alp Lusgen itself. Tyndall went to the Alps every summer from 1856 until his death in 1893, except for one year, 1891, when he was too ill to travel. These visits were his respite from the stresses of London life, and essential to restoring his mental equilibrium. Initially devoted to the exploration of glaciers, and then to mountaineering, Tyndall's sojourns recharged his batteries and gave him the deep contact with Nature that he craved. But they also gave him time to think and reflect at length. His major philosophical addresses to the British Association – Norwich in 1868, Liverpool in 1870 and

Belfast in 1874 – were conceived and largely written in the Alps, together with other articles and the editing of new editions of books. With these demands there was perhaps little time for poetry, at least until after his marriage to Louisa in 1876 and the almost immediate construction of the chalet on Alp Lusgen that then became their retreat. The death of Carlyle, in 1881, seems finally to have given the impetus for the production of this elegiac and revealing poem.

The archive at the Royal Institution holds 12 pages of handwritten drafts of the poem. It is evident that they relate only to the version published in 1881 and that the structure of the poem seems to have emerged quite fully formed from the outset. Nevertheless, the pages are littered with crossings-out, as two reasonably fair drafts emerge. The following critical lines required several drafts to crystallise:

> Whence the craft
> Which shook these gentian atoms into form,
> And dyed them with azure deeper far
> Than that of heaven itself on days serene?

A decade separates the early version from the final poem published as the last item in Tyndall's last book, *New Fragments*. In 1881, Tyndall was still in post at the Royal Institution and actively engaged in research. By 1892 he was retired, and a year from his untimely death. In those 10 years, Tyndall's sense of the Mystery, the Unknowable, as Spencer put it, seems only to have deepened. Talking to Tennyson in June 1890, Tyndall had remarked: 'God and Spirit I know, and matter I know; and I believe in both.' Then, in response to Tennyson's belief in individual immortality, he declared in pantheistic vein: 'We may all be absorbed into the Godhead.'[255] The way in which Tyndall revised the poem reveals the salient changes of emphasis in his beliefs.

The new version is tighter than the original 'rigmarole'. Compare the first eight lines of the original:

> The sun has cleared the hills, quenching the flush
> Of orient crimson with excess of light.
> The long grass quivers in the morning air
> Without a sound; yet each particular blade
> Hymns its own song, had we but ears to hear.
> The hot rays smite us, but a rhythmic breeze
> Keeps languor far away. Unslumbering,
> The eye and soul take in the mighty scene.

with those of the final version:

The sun has cleared the peaks and quenched the flush
Of orient crimson with excess of light.
The tall grass quivers in the rhythmic air
Without a sound; yet each particular blade
Trembles in song, had we but ears to hear.
The hot rays smite us, but a quickening breeze
Keeps languor far away. Unslumbering,
The soul enlarged takes in the mighty scene.

Not only is the metre firmer (though 'quenched the flush', despite being published initially as 'quenching the flush', appears in all the early drafts) but the imagery is also more vivid. 'Hills' become 'peaks'; the 'long grass' becomes the more melodic 'tall grass'; and the 'morning air' becomes the 'rhythmic air', as each blade now 'trembles in song' rather than 'hymns its own song'. The unseen wind, often suggesting inspiration in Romantic poetry, is rustling the grass, with echoes of Coleridge's 'Eolian Harp'. The unseen ether, pervading space, transmitting the 'hot rays' and 'excess of light', is also called to the imagination. The 'eye and soul' become the 'soul enlarged', as perception and feeling merge in a transcendental vision.

The poem turns on lines that have a clear echo of Emerson's 'The Rhodora: On being Asked, Whence the Flower'. This poem, written in 1834, explores the interconnectedness of Nature. Tyndall had invoked it before, in his lecture in 1867 on 'Matter and Force' to the working men at the British Association in Dundee, to express a sense of the reason for the existence of a beautiful flower:

Why thou wert there, O rival of the rose!
I never thought to ask, I never knew,
But in my simple ignorance supposed,
The self-same power that brought me here brought you.

This is the lecture, preceding the more famous Norwich Address of 1868, in which Tyndall argued that 'the physical philosopher, as such, must be a pure materialist'.[256] He went on to claim, in a striking passage: 'Depend upon it, if a chemist, by bringing the proper materials together in a retort or crucible, could make a baby, he would do it. There is no law, moral or physical, forbidding him to do it.'[257] The natural philosopher's researches should not be constrained, a theme he returned to more forcefully, and with far more public outcry, in the Belfast Address. But he went on to acknowledge the limits of science, recalling Napoleon's question to his savants as he looked aloft to the starry heavens and asked: '"but who made these?". That question still remains unanswered, and science makes no attempt to answer it. As far as I can see, there is no quality in the human intellect which is fit to be applied to the solution of the problem. It entirely transcends us.'[258] This sense remains in 'A morning on Alp Lusgen'.

'The Rhodora' would have had many resonances for Tyndall, not least in the rhododendron flower itself, conjuring images of the mountain azaleas, or Alpine roses, that surrounded him on Bel Alp. The wind or breeze summoned at the start of Tyndall's poem mirrors the 'sea-winds' of 'The Rhodora'. At the heart of his own poem, Tyndall asks in the initial version of 1881:

> Whence the craft
> Which shook these gentian atoms into form,
> And dyed them with azure deeper far
> Than that of heaven itself on days serene?
> What built these marigolds? What clothed these
> knolls
> With fiery bilberries? What gave the heath
> Its purple blossoms and the rose its glow?

His answer was Darwinian:

> Ah weary head! the answer is abroad,
> Buzzing through all the atmosphere of mind.
> 'Tis Evolution! East, West, North and South—
> From droughty sage and spinster shrill we learn
> 'Twas Evolution! When that word has spread
> Its magic to the limits of the world,
> Till its reverberation thence becomes
> A lullaby—how sweet 'twill be to doze
> Over thy emptied cup of nectar'd sweets
> Divine Philosophy!—To doze in peace.

This is less than a year before Darwin's death, which affected Tyndall greatly – he sat at the back of Westminster Abbey throughout the funeral service, head in hands. Tyndall regarded the theory of evolution as one of the great discoveries of the century and defended it on many visible platforms, not least in the Belfast Address of 1874. But, like Huxley, he was never entirely comfortable with natural selection, and a teleological sense does creep into his utterances. He felt some creative power, impenetrable to science – the Mystery that lay behind all.

By 1892, the Mystery has assumed a greater significance. Tyndall's question is subtly more fluent:

> Whence the craft
> Which shook these gentian atoms into form,
> And dyed the flower with azure deeper far
> Than that of heaven itself on days serene?
> What built these marigolds? What clothed these
> knolls
> With fiery whortle leaves? What gave the heath
> Its purple bloom—the Alpine rose its glow?

and the answer now is very different, with no mention of evolution:

> Shew us the power which fills each tuft of grass
> With sentient swarms?—the art transcending
> thought,
> Which paints against the canvas of the eye
> These crests sublime and pure, and then transmutes
> The picture into worship? Science dumb—
> Oh babbling Gnostic! cease to beat the air.
> We yearn, and grope, and guess, but cannot know.

Gone is even an attempt at a naturalistic explanation. There are some things beyond the powers of science to penetrate, and beyond human understanding.

The second part of the poem, from the line 'Low down, the yellow shingle of the Rhone', is more similar in sense in the two versions than the first part. For the 1892 version Tyndall adds three lines to his passage about Carlyle, to strengthen his case:

> Not for a monk your message; but for men
> With strength potential—leaders of the world
> Who took the truth you preached to set them free.

His implicit reference to Carlyle in the words 'Oh! sorrowing shade of him, who preached through life | Obedience to the Highest!' is footnoted with 'Carlyle' to make the reference clear. Tyndall did not do that in the 1881 version, perhaps because the allusion would have been obvious to most readers, following Carlyle's recent death.

Likewise, he adds five lines to the vivid picture of the landscape before him:

> Dom, Cervin—Weisshorn of the dazzling crown—
> Ye splendours of the Alps! Can earth elsewhere
> Bring forth a rival? Not the Indian chain,
> Though shouldered higher o'er the standard sea,
> Can front the eye with more majestic forms.

All three of those summits can be seen from Alp Lusgen. Tyndall had stood on two of them, the Cervin (Matterhorn) and the Weisshorn, but had been beaten back from the Dom, the highest mountain entirely in Switzerland, by inclement weather. He gives the 'dazzling crown' to the Weisshorn. Not only, perhaps, because he had made the first ascent but also because it is arguably the most beautiful of all the Alpine peaks, crowned with snow.

Then follows the final section of the poem, reflecting on the power of an idea, and the will, expressed through Napoleon: 'In one vast brain was born the motive power | Which swept whole armies over heights unscaled'. This question of consciousness and will, and how they could put in train vast physical forces, had exercised Tyndall since his youth. He could envisage no explanation in scientific terms.

The last 21 lines are identical in both versions, and the poem ends with a hymn to Carlyle:

> Oh, shade before invoked,
> You spoke of Might and Right; and many a shaft
> Barbed with the sneer, 'He preaches force—brute force,'
> Has rattled on your shield. But well you knew
> Might, to be Might, must base itself on Right,
> Or vanish evanescent as the deeds
> Of France's Emperor. Reflect on this,
> Ye temporary darlings of the crowd.
> To-day ye may have peans in your ears;
> To-morrow ye lie rotten, if your work
> Lack that true core which gives to Right and Might
> One meaning in the end.

Gregory Tate comments on this poem:

> There is no certain recourse to a Christian God or an intelligent 'will' in 'A morning on Alp Lusgen'. The poem pursues its search for origins from the perspective of scientific naturalism, tracing the movement of material atoms from stars to the 'Alpine rose.' Yet this atomic model is not, for Tyndall, reductive or mechanistic: in typical Romantic fashion, Tyndall's poem celebrates the beauty of flowers and forests and the sublimity of mountains. It also evokes the sublimity of the scientific theory of the stellar origin of matter, while at the same time acknowledging the limits of scientific knowledge.[259]

Materialism could only take him so far. The rest was unknowable.

In Tyndall's poetry we have a window into his soul. It expresses his personal and emotional life as a young man, valuing his male friends and exploring his interactions and romances with women, and reflects his progression as he matured as a natural philosopher and established himself as a man of science. His love poems take us from his early forays into romance to a mature and platonic loving relationship with an accomplished married woman. His humour is both delightful and at times excruciating, depending on taste. His social assumptions about class and gender are forthrightly displayed. Further, his sweeping philosophy, transcending his deeply felt perceptions of landscape to embrace a perceived holistic universe, is laid out in the poems, culminating in the manifesto of 'A morning on Alp Lusgen'.

As for its purpose for Tyndall himself, poetry allowed him to open his soul, his aesthetic and romantic sense, to sensibility. It was the means by which he communicated to dear friends and reviewed his own emotional and aesthetic response to landscape and to love. He read the 'greats', and this reading and his poetic compositions were part of his development as a learned and cultured man who could take what he regarded as his rightful place in society and speak evocatively to packed lecture halls and formal gatherings. His early poetry was part of his youthful self-fashioning, and was largely put aside as his scientific explorations and institutional commitments consumed his time. Yet he continued to use poetic expression in his prose writings about science – the 'poet of science' indeed. 'A morning on Alp Lusgen' shows his resort to the pure medium as he laid out his philosophy at the end of his life.

Notes

1 Tyndall 1864, 726.
2 See Holmes 2012.
3 Jeans 1887, 73.
4 Barton, Rankin and Reidy 2017, 445.
5 See e.g. DeYoung 2011; Elwick, Jackson, Lightman and Reidy 2016–; Jackson 2018; Barton 2018.
6 See e.g. Jenkins 2007; Beer 2009; Brown 2013; Herapath and Mason 2015; Holmes and Ruston 2017; Illingworth 2019; McLeish 2019; Tate 2020.
7 See Morrell and Thackray 1981; MacLeod and Collins 1981.
8 Huxley 1894, 5–6.
9 See e.g. Beer 2009; Gold 2010; Brown 2013; Pratt-Smith 2014.
10 Poem 61.
11 Poem 76.
12 Poem 12.
13 Poems 7 and 18.
14 Poem 10.
15 Poem 29.
16 Poem 28.
17 Poem 76.
18 Mackowiak 2006, 41.
19 Letter from John Tyndall to Mary Ann Coxe, 4 October 1866, RI MS JT/1/T/251. The excerpt is from *Childe Harold's Pilgrimage: The Night before the Battle of Waterloo*.
20 Eve and Creasey 1945, 286–7.
21 Letter from Louisa Tyndall to Dr Hutchinson, c.1893, RI MS LT/14/29.
22 Letter from John Tyndall to Burchell, [6] August 1842. See Cantor and Dawson 2016, 253. See Byron. 1816. *The Siege of Corinth*, xi. 248–51.
23 Letter from John Tyndall to William Ginty, 29 July 1844. See Baldwin and Browne 2016, 207. See Browning. 1826. 'An Essay on Mind', verses 69–70.
24 Letter from John Tyndall to Jack Tidmarsh, 14 July 1845. See Baldwin and Browne 2016, 234. This is probably a translation from Goethe's *Faust*, 3136–7: 'Meine Ruh ist hin, | Mein Herz ist schwer.'
25 Tyndall Journal, RI MS JT/1/13a/55. See Byron. *Don Juan*, canto xv, stanza 99.
26 Tyndall Journal, RI MS JT/1/13a/55. The quote is from Goethe's 'The Mason Lodge' in a translation by Thomas Carlyle.
27 Tyndall Journal, RI MS JT/1/13a/151. The quote is from Wordsworth's 'It is a Beauteous Evening, Calm and Free'. The poem begins: 'It is a beauteous evening, calm and free | The holy time is quiet as a Nun | Breathless with adoration; the broad sun | Is sinking down in its tranquility;'.
28 Tyndall Journal, RI MS JT/1/13a/197. See Shelley. *Queen Mab*, canto ix, stanza 5 and canto vi, stanza 8.
29 Jackson 2018, 110.
30 Poem 2.
31 Poem 3.
32 Poem 4.
33 Poem 5.
34 Harvey 1814, II. xv. 8.
35 See DeArce, McGing and McMillan 2013–14.
36 Poem 44.
37 Hesketh 2019, 460.
38 Tyndall Journal, RI MS JT/2/13b/512.
39 Lightman 2015.
40 Poem 65.
41 See Hevly 1996.
42 Poems 53 and 54.
43 Poem 65.
44 Poem 57.

45 Poem 60.
46 Poem 63.
47 Poem 28.
48 Poem 74.
49 Poems 16 and 28.
50 Poem 30.
51 Poems 66 and 35.
52 Poems 26 and 27.
53 Poem 58.
54 Poem 47.
55 Poems 29 and 13.
56 Poem 14.
57 Poem 61.
58 Poem 72.
59 Poem 42.
60 Poem 17.
61 Poem 30.
62 Beer 2009, 64–5.
63 Poem 61.
64 Poem 53.
65 Poem 59.
66 Poem 65.
67 *Belfast News-Letter* (12 February 1890), 7.
68 Poem 17.
69 Poem 13.
70 Beer 2009, 64–5.
71 Poem 13.
72 Poem 53.
73 Poem 32.
74 Poem 34.
75 Tucker 1996, 158.
76 Blake 1793, quoted in Tucker 1996, 158.
77 Tucker writes of how figurative images of soul in poetry are anarchic revealers of unconscious positions, particularly concerning the mind/body dialectic; they are 'apt inspection sites for evidence of cultural contestation'. An unusual image of soul, such as in Elizabeth Barrett Browning's line 'the rank saliva of her soul' from her 'Bianca Among the Nightingales' (1860), exerts just such a shock to standard conceptions of soul: it 'anatomizes its inconsistencies'. Tucker 1996, 159.
78 This is taken from Robert Browning's *Fra Lippo Lippi*, ii 183–5. The poem was first published in 1855 and is cited in Tucker 1996, 157.
79 Tucker 1996, 163.
80 Letter from John Tyndall to Juliet Pollock, [16 April 1862], RI MS JT/1/T/1136, cited in Mackowiak 2006, 15. See letter 1885 in Finnegan, Jackson and Kaalund 2019, 424.
81 Tyndall 1870a, 3.
82 Tyndall 1870a, 37.
83 Quinney 2009, 22.
84 Tucker 1996, 169.
85 Tucker 1996, 169.
86 Tucker 1996, 168.
87 Poem 76.
88 Tyndall 1870a, 25.
89 Tucker 1996, 159.
90 Poem 68.
91 Poem 68.
92 Poem 30.
93 Poem 10.
94 Poem 11.
95 Poem 11.

96 Poem 53.
97 Poem 56.
98 Poem 47.
99 Poem 11.
100 Opie and Opie 1952, 101. See also Opie and Opie 1955, 69.
101 Poem 47.
102 Poem 18.
103 Ballard 1990, 107.
104 Poem 33.
105 Poem 15.
106 Poem 18.
107 Poem 65.
108 Poem 16.
109 Poem 24.
110 Poem 25.
111 Poem 28.
112 Poem 12.
113 Poem 11.
114 Poem 16.
115 Poem 12.
116 Poem 37.
117 Poems 12 and 30.
118 Poem 18.
119 See poem 13, n. 1, and poem 27, n. 2.
120 Poem 18.
121 Poem 22.
122 Jackson 2018, 16.
123 Poem 18.
124 Poem 20.
125 Poem 74.
126 Poem 9.
127 Poem 42.
128 Poem 44.
129 Poem 53.
130 Poem 56.
131 Beer 2009, 84.
132 Beer 2009, 4.
133 Poem 56.
134 Poems 17, 18 and 19.
135 Poem 18.
136 Mary Edwards; see poem 12, an unfortunate prank given that Mary had just become engaged to another in perfect propriety.
137 Poem 18.
138 Poem 16.
139 Poem 20.
140 Poem 56.
141 RI MS JT/2/13c/1020.
142 RI MS JT/3/23/26–9.
143 Poem 11.
144 Poem 24.
145 Jackson 2018, 144–5.
146 Poem 24.
147 Poem 28.
148 Spenser, 1594.
149 Poem 28.
150 Published as 'Effusion XXXV' in Coleridge 1796, 96–100.
151 Letter from John Tyndall to Juliet Pollock, 4 September 1871, RI MS JT/1/T/1154.
152 Poem 35.

153 Poem 28.
154 Russett 1989, 80.
155 Richards 2017, 482.
156 Poem 33.
157 Alexander 1850, 27.
158 Poem 35.
159 Poem 70.
160 Sørensen 2015, 69.
161 Sørensen 2015, 69.
162 Poem 72.
163 Brown 2013, 159.
164 Trowbridge 2018, 8.
165 Trowbridge 2018, 47.
166 Cited in Trowbridge 2018, 40.
167 Mackowiak 2006, 187.
168 Poem 75.
169 Brown 2013, 161.
170 Tyndall 1860, 163–4.
171 Bartlett 1995, cited in Mackowiak 2006, 159.
172 Letter from John Tyndall to Michael Faraday, 27 December 1859, RI MS JT/1/TYP/12/4100. See Finnegan, Jackson and Kaalund 2019, 122.
173 Mackowiak 2006, 184–5.
174 Poem 74.
175 Mackowiak 2006, 184.
176 Milton 1645, 13–14.
177 Letter from Juliet Pollock to John Tyndall, RI MS JT/1/P/212; RI MS JT/1/TYP/6/2118.
178 Letter from John Tyndall to L. Darmstaedter, 7 October 1887, SB Slg Darmstaedter 1855 Tyndall Be. 10–11.
179 Tyndall Journal, RI MS JT/2/13a/i–ii.
180 Tyndall Journal, RI MS JT/2/13a/iii–xi.
181 Wat Ripton. 'The German Student', *Preston Chronicle* (24 February 1849).
182 Wat Ripton. 'Excursion into Germany' and 'A Whitsuntide Ramble', *Preston Chronicle* (19 May 1849 and 16 June 1849).
183 See 'Turner translates Carnot', in Serres 1982, 54–64.
184 Poem 59.
185 Wat Ripton. 'Sisters of the Rhine', *Preston Chronicle* (3, 10, 17, 24 November and 1 December 1849).
186 Wat Ripton. 'Man and Magnetism', *Preston Chronicle* (9 March 1850); Wat Ripton. 'Zig-Zag', *Preston Chronicle* (20 April 1850); Wat Ripton. 'Day Book Splinters', *Preston Chronicle* (13 July 1850); Wat Ripton. 'Association and Speculation', *Preston Chronicle* (10 August 1850).
187 Wat Ripton. 'Zig-Zag', *Preston Chronicle* (20 April 1850).
188 Shelley 1840, 9. The essay was written in 1821.
189 Henry Bence Jones to Emil du Bois-Reymond, 5 April 1869.
190 Letter from John Tyndall to Michael Faraday, 26 December 1859, in Finnegan, Jackson and Kaalund 2019, 118; original version in Tyndall Journal (25 December 1859), RI MS JT/2/13c/1168–9.
191 Tyndall 1906, xi.
192 Tyndall 1906, 29. Like much of Tyndall's writing about the mountains, in letters, articles and books, this piece is reworked from a journal entry which ends differently but just as evocatively: 'Long after night set in a ghostly gleam of white light rested upon the summit of the Ortler. The snow slopes behind on the contrary had a blue tinge, onward in the distance the summits deepened into a dusky neutral tint and were finally lost in space' (Tyndall Journal, 5 September 1856, RI MS JT/2/13c/900).
193 Letter from John Tyndall to Richard Dawes, 18 December 1860, RI MS JT/1/TYP/1/320a–320b.
194 Sylvester made these remarks in his Presidential Address to the Mathematical and Physical Section of the British Association for the Advancement of Science in Exeter in 1869, following Tyndall's Address in Norwich in 1868. The address was reproduced in Sylvester 1870, 103.

195 Letter from John Tyndall to Thomas Hirst, 13 July 1850, RI MS JT/1/T/529. See Barton, Rankin and Reidy 2017, 77.

196 Letter from John Tyndall to Thomas Hirst, 19 August 1850, RI MS 1/T/532. See Barton, Rankin and Reidy 2017, 120. The quote is from Alexander Pope's 'An Essay on Man': Epistle I (1733), section IX, lines 9–10.

197 Tyndall 1862, 1.

198 The remaining epigraphs are as follows:

Chapter 2 'Meyringen to the Grimsel', from Emerson's 'The World-Soul', as he pictures the familiar landscape:

Spring still makes spring in the mind
When sixty years are told,
Love wakes anew this throbbing heart,
And we are never old.
Over the winter glaciers
I see the summer glow,
And through the wild-piled snow drift
The warm rose buds below.

Chapter 3 (The Grimsel and Aeggishorn), from 'Monadnoc', as the cliffs lour over him:

Thou trowest
How the chemic eddies play
Pole to pole, and what they say;
And that these gray crags
Not on crags are hung,
But beads are of a rosary
On prayer and music strung.

Chapter 4 (Bel Alp), from 'Monadnoc', about the place that would become his Alpine home:

Happy, I said, whose home is here;
Fair fortunes to the Mountaineer.

Chapter 5 (Reflections), from 'Monadnoc' (see also below):

The world was made in order,
And the atoms march in tune.

Chapter 6 (Ascent of the Weisshorn), from 'Monadnoc', as Tyndall holds himself up as a 'finer spirit', ascending the previously 'unploughed' summit:

In his own loom's garment drest,
By his proper bounty blest,
Fast abides this constant giver,
Pouring many a cheerful river,
To far eyes an aërial isle,
Unploughed, which finer spirits pile;
Which morn, and crimson evening, paint
For bard, for lover, and for saint;
The country's core,
Inspirer, prophet, evermore!

Chapter 7 (The Descent), from Tennyson's 'The Eagle', expressing the physicality of mountaineering:

He clasps the crag with hooked hands.

Chapter 8 (The Motion of Glaciers), from Emerson's 'Ode to William H. Channing', perhaps a self-awareness of Tyndall's insignificance against the peaks and glaciers:

The god that made New Hampshire,
Taunted the lofty land
With little men.

Chapter 9 (Sunrise on the Pines), from Emerson's 'Woodnotes II':

> The sunbeam gave me to the sight
> The tree adorned the formless light.

Chapter 10 (Inspection of the Matterhorn), from 'Monadnoc', redolent of the colossal Matterhorn:

> By million changes skilled to tell
> What in the Eternal standeth well,
> And what obedient Nature can,
> Is this colossal talisman.

Chapter 11 (Over the Moro), from Tennyson's 'The Princess'. The Monte Moro pass, between Macugnaga and Saas, traverses past precipices, peaks, a lake and waterfalls:

> The splendour falls on rocky walls
> And snowy summits old in story,
> The long light shakes across the lakes,
> And the wild cataract leaps in glory.

Chapter 12 (The Old Weissthor), from Tennyson's 'St Agnes' Eve', evoking this narrow gateway pass, high in the snows:

> He lifts me to the golden doors
> The flashes come and go;
> All heaven bursts her starry floors
> And strows her light below.

199 See e.g. 'Voyage to Algiers', in Tyndall 1879, vol. 1, 217; 'Niagara', in Tyndall 1879, vol. 1, 231; 'Old Alpine Jottings', in Tyndall 1892, 435, 437, 464 and 466.
200 Tyndall 1862, 1.
201 Tyndall 1862, 2.
202 See 'Matter and Force', in Tyndall 1879, vol. 2, 66.
203 Ruskin 1905.
204 Ruskin 1893, xvii.
205 See Jackson 2018, 254–5.
206 A slight misquote, as the poem runs: 'The world was built in order'.
207 See https://drgregorytate.wordpress.com/2015/11/30/the-uses-of-poetry-in-victorian-science/ (accessed 30 January 2020).
208 Tyndall 1863, 433.
209 Choi 2007, 314.
210 See Smith, Jonathan, 'Writing Science: Scientific Prose', in Holmes and Ruston 2017, 141–54.
211 Haugrud 1970.
212 Tyndall 1870a, 13–51.
213 Tyndall 1870a, 20.
214 Wat Ripton. 'Goethe and Faust', *Preston Chronicle* (29 September 1849), 3.
215 Tyndall Journal, 21 June 1855, RI MS JT/2/13c/751.
216 Tyndall 1870b, 62.
217 Tyndall 1870b, 63.
218 Tyndall 1870b, 65.
219 Clifford 1879, vol. 1, 1.
220 Clifford 1879, vol. 2, 255.
221 Tyndall to Juliet Pollock, 15 August 1857, in Barton, Browne, Corbett and McMillan 2018, 207. The phrase 'Nature never did betray the heart that loved her' is taken from William Wordsworth's 1798 poem 'Lines Written a Few Miles Above Tintern Abbey, on revisiting the Banks of the Wye During a Tour', in Wordsworth's *Lyrical Ballads* (London: J. and A. Arch, 1798).
222 Spencer 1861, 81–2.
223 John Tyndall to unknown, 27 December 1876, Wellcome Library MS. 7777/19.
224 John Tyndall to unknown (Lady Welby?), 16 February ny, Wellcome Library MS. 7777/43.
225 Tyndall 1892, 77.

226 Poem 59.
227 Poem 12.
228 Tyndall 1879, vol. 2, 241.
229 See Tate, Gregory, 'Poetry and Science', in Holmes and Ruston 2017, 101–14.
230 Wordsworth 1802, xxxvii. John Stuart Mill, whom Tyndall greatly admired, had written in similar vein: 'The object of poetry is confessedly to act upon the emotions; and therein is poetry sufficiently distinguished from what Wordsworth affirms to be its logical opposite, namely, not prose, but matter of fact or science.' See Mill 1833, 60–1. The essay is reprinted in Herapath and Mason 2015, 73–80, quote on 73.
231 Poem 68.
232 See, for example, Turner 1993, 262–83.
233 We are grateful to Gregory Tate for sight of an unpublished paper touching on these points, further addressed in his recent book (Tate 2020). See https://drgregorytate.wordpress.com/2017/09/13/nineteenth-century-poetry-and-the-physical-sciences/amp/ (accessed 4 February 2020). Gowan Dawson and Sally Shuttleworth note that scientists 'made use of the enormous cultural authority of Victorian poetry to reinforce, as well as add respectability to, their often controversial scientific arguments'; see Dawson and Shuttleworth 2003, 9.
234 Tyndall 1870a, 48.
235 'What were the God who sat outside to scan

> The spheres that 'neath his finder circling ran?
> God dwells within, and moves the world and moulds,
> Himself and Nature in one form enfolds:'

From *The Spectator*, 24 September 1870, quoted in Tyndall 1870a, 9.
236 Tyndall 1872a, 417–18.
237 Tyndall 1892, 46.
238 Tyndall 1879, vol. 2, 371, 373.
239 Tyndall 1863, 360.
240 Tyndall 1867, 33. The quote is from Tennyson's *Morte d'Arthur*:

> 'In those old days, one summer noon, an arm
> Rose up from out the bosom of the lake,
> Clothed in white samite, mystic, wonderful,
> Holding the sword—and how I row'd across
> And took it, and have worn it, like a king:'

241 Tyndall 1867, 33. The quote is from Emerson's 'The Gypsy Trail'.
242 Poem 76.
243 See e.g. O'Gorman 1997; Mackowiak 2006; Brown 2013.
244 O'Gorman 1997, 353.
245 Tyndall 1892, 498–500.
246 Mackowiak 2006, 170.
247 Brown 2013, 158.
248 Letter from John Tyndall to Thomas Hirst, 9 August 1881, BL Add MS 53716, 172–172a.
249 O'Gorman 1997, 353.
250 Brown 2013, 160.
251 Mackowiak 2006, 169–71.
252 See e.g. 'Matter and Force', in Tyndall 1879, vol. 2, 73.
253 Herapath and Mason 2015, 250.
254 Tyndall 1865.
255 Tennyson 1897, vol. 2, 380.
256 Tyndall 1879, vol. 2, 72.
257 Tyndall 1879, vol. 2, 72.
258 Tyndall 1879, vol. 2, 73.
259 Tate, Gregory. 'The Poetry of Scientists', https://drgregorytate.wordpress.com/2014/10/21/the-poetry-of-scientists/ (blogpost, accessed 30 January 2020).

John Tyndall

The poems

1 Acrostic (Maria)[1] 1840

M–ay heaven its choicest holiest blessings strew
A–nd beam its purest, brightest rays on you
R–est sweet one rest devoid of care or dread
I–ncense the balmiest on thy path be shed
A–nd seraphs watch around thy peaceful bed

RI MS JT/3/42/15[2]

1 Possibly Maria Payne, his cousin, who wrote quite intimately to Tyndall.
2 There is a second version at RI MS JT/8/2/1/11, dated Youghal 1840.

2 [In praise of Bruen][1] 22 July 1841[2]

Let fame her golden trumpet sound
Let Erin[3] join the theme
And Barrow's beauteous banks[4] resound
In praise of Bruen's name.
You deem me an enthusiast, but
'Breathes there a man with a soul so dead
That never to himself hath said
This is my own native land'.[5]

RI MS JT/1/10/3232[6]
Typewritten transcript only

1 This is written in a letter to his father (see n. 6), following the victory of the Conservative candidates Colonel Henry Bruen and Thomas Bunbury in the 1841 General Election for County Carlow. See also 'The testimonial' (poem 5). Bruen (1789–1852) resided on the family's Oak Park Estate on the northern outskirts of Carlow and was the colonel of the Carlow Regiment of Militia. A wealthy Protestant, Tory landowner and man of influence, he represented Carlow County in Parliament from 1812 until 1831 and then stood again in 1835, but the result was contested. He returned to Parliament later that year after a contested by-election but was defeated in the General Election of 1837. He won a by-election in December 1840, following the death of the standing Liberal MP, and was re-elected at the General Election in July 1841.
2 Tyndall was in Kinsale, working for the Irish Ordnance Survey.
3 *Erin*: romantic name for Ireland.
4 *Barrow's beauteous banks*: the River Barrow, which flows through Carlow.
5 *Breathes there … native land*: Walter Scott, *The Last Lay of the Minstrel* (1805), VI.i.1–3.
6 See also John Tyndall to his father, 22 July 1841 (letter 0080, TC1). Annotations to this poem are derived from this letter.

3 The Leighlin "Orators"—or, 'The late repeal meeting'[1] 12 October 1841[2]

What sounds are these which strong and clear
Strike full upon my ravished ear?
'Tis freedom—bursting from the night
Of ages, sheds her glorious light
O'er Erin's[3] undulating plains
Her cloud-capped hills and mouldering fanes!
List![4] Carlow list! while young ONeill[5]
Vociferated—Repeal!—Repeal![6]
Hark! rising to the shrilling cry,
The voice of Leighlin answers nigh.
See! as the swelling notes ascend
The poplars on the Bawnague[7] bend!
And echo wafts it far and wide;
Along the Barrow's[8] placid tide.
And hark! along the eastern line,
The 'Captain's'[9] geese in cackle join
In council sworn—every one
To help their brother of the Swan*
With tail erect in wild amaze,
Each hungry ass in concert brays!
And had they Baalam's gift[10] you'd hear
Them give their fellow ass a cheer
Oh! who can con the glorious theme
Nor glow with all a patriot's flame?
Strike! Erin Strike! the happy lyre,
Your Sons have caught the gen'rous fire;
And Tory Bruen[11] waxes pale
Before the doughty young O'Neill;
And Tory tyrants now confess
This youth the lustre of the press.—
And Tim[12] honoured in modern Story,
(Sure youthful hearts will pant for glory)
From young ambition's gleaming pyre
Has snatched the title of 'Esquire'!
A man of stalwart consequence,
Though some assert a lackbrained fool,
The deadly foe of common sense
The wise man's scoff—the villain's tool

A bubble-full of empty pride,
The filth of agitation's foam,
That drops into oblivion's tide
'Unwept – unhonoured – and unknown'.[13]
Oh! is it then such [pulling] things
That Erin's dignity maintains?
Ah no!—each apish essay flings
A deeper tint upon her stains
Presumptions Jackanapes!—resign
Your tiny pens to other hands
Fulfill your destiny's design
Go mete the tape and measure drams!
Nor once again vain fools aspire
Beyond the counters genial noise,
In scorn my glowing thoughts expire
Goodbye ye patriotic boys!—

*the Swan hotel

RI MS JT 8/2/1/1–2[14]
Typewritten transcript only

1 Written under the pseudonym W. S. (Walter Snooks). DeArce, McGing and McMillan (2013–14) suggest that this is a reference to the nationalist romanticism of Sir Walter Scott as an inspiration.
2 Tyndall was in Kinsale, working for the Irish Ordnance Survey. The poem was published in *The Carlow Sentinel*, 16 October 1841, [3]. The published version has different punctuation in places.
3 *Erin's*: romantic name for Ireland.
4 *List!*: listen.
5 *young ONeill*: the son of Terence O'Neill, of the Swan Inn hotel, Leighlinbridge, who had written two letters about the Repeal of the Union (see letter 0098, TC1).
6 *Repeal!*: referring to the movement led by Daniel O'Connell (1775–1847) to repeal the Act of Union of 1800 between Great Britain and Ireland.
7 *Bawnague*: probably Bawnogue or Bownoge, near Baltinglass, about 12 miles north-west of Carlow.
8 *Barrow's*: the River Barrow, which flows through Leighlinbridge.
9 *'Captain's'*: probably Captain Thomas Woodcock (see letters 0066 and 0090, TC1).
10 *Baalam's gift*: the gift of prophecy (Numbers 22: 1–3).
11 *Bruen*: see poem 2, n. 1.
12 *Tim*: either Timothy Hennessy or Terence O'Neill's son, both mentioned earlier in the letter 0101, TC1.
13 *'Unwept – unhonoured – and unknown'*: misquotation of 'Unwept, unhonoured, and unsung' in Walter Scott, *The Lay of the Last Minstrel* (1805), VI.i.16.
14 See also John Tyndall to Editor of *The Carlow Sentinel*, 12 October 1841 (letter 0101, TC1). Annotations to this poem are derived from this letter.

4 Carlow[1] 26 October 1841[2]

Sweet spot! where first th'imperfect accent hung
In lingering lispings on my infant tongue
Where young imagination first took flight
And roam'd unshackled thro' the realms of light,
When bright and happy life's perspective shone
And golden vistas opened farther on
Each dancing stream that woos the Suns bright rays
Each wee wild flower that blossoms on thy braes
Each shrub that sheds its fragrance in the dell
Around my soul has cast a hallowed spell—
Sweet blissful spot! where Barrow fair and free
Rolls liquid chrystal to the distant sea[3]
Fall oft when morning tinged the orient sky
And heav'ns calm azure spread itself on high
I've trod thy banks in summer beauty drest
T'inhale the breeze that freshened o'er thy breath
And when from Zenith fall the scorching ray
In reckless frolic gambolled with thy spray
Ere sanguine strife thy hollows had bestained
Or friendships mourned her Sacred Courts profaned
Her glimmering incense cheered each passing gloom
The heart its altar—union its perfume
Oh then approving heavens smiled to see
Congenial bosoms throb in sympathy
Alas how changed, these Halcyon days are o'er
And drooping Carlow must their loss deplore
Now agitation whelms her like a flood
And noisome vermin* gloat upon her blood
Where peace sat smilingly gloomy terror reigns
And Ate[4] revels o'er thy lovely plains
Discords black banner now each Zephyr fills
And darkly hovering o'er thy sunny hills
Each cloudlet big with desolation hangs
While reeking 'neath O'Connell's[5] vampyre fangs
Prostrate you lie—each burning tear that's shed
Calls down damnation on his guilty head
What tho' the fiat linger on the tongue
of Justice—tho' the hair-held sword has hung
So long above thee waiting the decree

of slumbering vengeance to descend on thee
Tho' Titan-like you raise your impious hand
And brandish in high heav'ns face your brand
Thy day arrives—the widow's withering ban[6]
Shall burst in thunders o'er thee—bloody man.
Nor lost to fame in ages yet to come
Fell infamy still brood upon thy tongue
And execution grim shall mark the spot
Where low you lie—detested not forgot

*Bugs &c.

RI MS JT 8/2/1/3–4[7]
Typewritten transcript only

1 Written under the pseudonym W. S. (Walter Snooks).
2 Tyndall was in Kinsale, working for the Irish Ordnance Survey. The poem was published in *The Carlow Sentinel*, 30 October 1841, [3]. The published version has different punctuation in places.
3 *Barrow fair and free | Rolls liquid chrystal to the distant sea*: the River Barrow flows through Carlow to Waterford Bay.
4 *Ate*: Atë, in Greek mythology, is the goddess of mischief, delusion, ruin and folly.
5 *O'Connell's*: Daniel O'Connell, see poem 3, n. 6.
6 *the widow's withering ban*: in 1815 Daniel O'Connell had killed John D'Esterre, a member of the Dublin Corporation, in a duel. His widow Jane Lucretia D'Esterre (1797–1868) angrily refused O'Connell's remorseful offer to share his income with her, although she did accept an annuity to support her daughter. A ban is an imprecation of a curse, an execration or malediction expressing anger (*OED*).
7 See also John Tyndall to Editor of *The Carlow Sentinel*, 26 October 1841 (letter 0106, TC1). Annotations to this poem are derived from this letter.

5 The testimonial[1] 8 November 1841[2]

Hark the voice of empire calls
Forward to the Shrine of fame
on its cloud crown'd capitals
Emblazon Bruen's[3] name

Lo the answering signal brand
Flashes on Mononia's[4] rills
Gleaming bright from strand to strand
Sheds its light on Ullin's hills[5]

As turns the Moslem to the shrine
When the last tinges of the sun
In all their golden glory shine
Above the distant horizon
Each grateful eye is burned on thee*
Hibernia's new Thermopylae[6]

The soaring condor plumes his wing
on Chimborazo's lofty peak[7]
And hears the mountain echoes ring
In dread explosion far beneath
Amid the elemental war
The Spirit of the tempest rides
And flashing from his cloudy car
Red lightnings hiss along the mountain's sides
Unmoved—unruffled and serene
The tenant of the crag looks down upon the scene

So stood brave Bruen undisturb'd he viewed
The scowling cloud of agitation lour
With steady eye—his lofty brow unmoved
He calmly waited the impending shower
And when at length the demon of the storm
Let loose the thunders from his red right hand
The dauntless chief on freedom's pinions borne
Unfurled her flag and drew her flaming brand
And mantling on his cheek the patriots glow
He hurled defiance at his gorgon[8] foe

And oft to battle for the right
He led his trusty men
And oft was worsted in the fight
Yet Brucelike[9] fought again

And conquered too—the wild hurrah
Has reached the distant sky
And echo from her mountain hold
Has answered cry for cry

Tho' rent by many an adverse breeze
Upon the battle plain
His glorious banner freely waves
Unsullied by a stain

While surpliced fiends[10]—Hell's viper spawn
Before the standard bow
Lerne[11] twines the laurel wreath
To bind the champions brow.

Now the voice of empire calls
Forward to the shrine of flame
On its cloud crowned capital
Emblazon Bruen's name

*Carlow

RI MS JT 8/2/1/5–6[12]
Typewritten transcript only

1 Written under the pseudonym W. S. (Walter Snooks).
2 Tyndall was in Kinsale, working for the Irish Ordnance Survey. The poem was published in *The Carlow Sentinel*, 13 November 1841, [3]. The published version has different punctuation in places.
3 *Bruen's*: see poem 2, n. 1.
4 *Mononia's*: Mononia is the Province of Munster, comprising Counties Clare, Cork, Kerry, Limerick, Tipperary and Waterford. The principal source for 'Mononia' was the poem 'Remember the Glories of Brien the Brave' in Thomas Moore's *Irish Melodies* (1821).
5 *Ullin's hills*: 'And Ullin's hills be silent as the grave' (G. Harvey, trans., *Ossian's Fingal: A Ancient Epic Poem* (London: Valpy, 1814), II.xv.8).

6 *Hibernia's new Thermopylae*: Colonel Henry Bruen's electoral success at Carlow in 1841 is here compared with the famous battle at Thermopylae in 480 BCE, when the Greek forces repelled a far larger army of Persian soldiers. Hibernia is the Classical Latin name for Ireland.

7 *Chimborazo's lofty peak*: one of the highest mountains in the Andes in South America and the highest mountain in Ecuador at 6,263 m (20,549 ft).

8 *gorgon*: in Greek mythology the Gorgons were three sisters whose hair was made from venomous snakes and who turned those who looked at them into stone.

9 *Brucelike*: The Scottish warrior king, Robert the Bruce (1274–1329), defeated a far larger English army at the Battle of Bannockburn in 1314. He later invaded Ireland to assist the Irish struggle against England.

10 *surpliced fiends*: wearing the loose vestment of white linen worn over a cassock by Roman Catholic priests.

11 *Lerne*: possibly the Lernaean Hydra that, in Greek mythology, was a many-headed serpent.

12 See also John Tyndall to Editor of *The Carlow Sentinel* (letter 0110, TC1). Annotations to this poem are derived from this letter.

6 The battle of the constitution is to be fought at the registry[1] 27 November 1841[2]

Child of the North![3]—the fairest scene for thee
The native mountains' wild sublimity
Which proudly from their kindred clouds look down,
White snows eternal form their dazzling crown,
Thou lov'st to see the foaming Geyser rise,
Bounding from earth in mingle with the skies;
And tho' the truant feet may widely roam,
The fondest thoughts still linger round thy home.
Thus, Carlow, thus—wheree'er my lot may be,
Fond mem'ry clings tenaciously to thee!

Hail! thou theme of wide-spread story,
  Well and bravely hast thou done;
Snatched the mead of dreadful glory.
  "IRELAND'S BATTLE" fought and won![4]

Shall the harp of Erin[5] slumber
  On the Oak—a silent thing?
Wake, Oh wake! the tuneful number,
  Strike! Oh strike! the golden string!

When carpet lords ignobly hung
  On ladies eyes from day to day,
Thy gallant son[6]—the fearless "ONE"*
  Pronounced the fiat—"Serfs away!"

The icy shackles of the tomb
  Of ten years growth are burst, and now;
A ray from heav'n dispels the gloom
  Which darkened o'er the nation's brow.

Old Scoted[7] gazed, and shrill and clear
  Her thrilling pibroch[8] then did blaw,
And hoary Lomond[9] stooped to hear
  The joyous notes of Whigs awa'!

When once the conquering eagle rose,

With purple wing above the slain,
As havock sheathed his reeking sword,
Upon Pharsalia's bloody plain.[10]

Did Caesar linger? Shadowy bands
Of crimson Munda,[11] is it so?
Resounding o'er her arid lands,
The voice of Sybia[12] answers; 'No.'

Men of Carlow! Now's the time;
Rush to the embattled walls,
Writhing in his filthy slime
Crush the Hydra[13] as she sprawls!

Onward! spirits of the free
Join the glorious Spartan[14] band;
Let your thrilling watchword be;
'BRUEN and our native land!'

*O'Connell gives him this honour.

Carlow Sentinel, 27 November 1841, [3]
Typewritten transcript only

1 Written under the pseudonym W. S. (Walter Snooks).
2 Tyndall was in Kinsale, working for the Irish Ordnance Survey. The poem was published in *The Carlow Sentinel*, 27 November 1841, [3]. For a commentary on this poem, see DeArce, McGing and McMillan (2013–14).
3 *Child of the North!*: according to DeArce, McGing and McMillan (2013–14) this refers to a specific section of the voting population of Carlow.
4 *"IRELAND'S BATTLE" fought and won!*: in the General Election of 1841, the Conservatives Colonel Henry Bruen and Thomas Bunbury had beaten Liberals (Whigs) in both County Carlow seats.
5 *harp of Erin*: traditional Irish symbol.
6 *Thy gallant son*: Henry Bruen, as revealed in the final line. See poem 2, n. 1.
7 *Old Scoted*: presumably a Scottish reference.
8 *pibroch*: a form of martial or funerary music for the bagpipes.
9 *hoary Lomond*: Ben Lomond, a mountain in the Scottish Highlands.
10 *Pharsalia's bloody plain*: in the Battle of Pharsalus in 48 BCE, a decisive battle in Caesar's Civil War, Caesar defeated Pompey.
11 *Munda*: the Battle of Munda in 45 BCE, in Spain, was the final conflict in the Civil War, in which Caesar defeated the forces of Pompey.
12 *voice of Sybia*: reference unclear.
13 *Hydra*: see poem 5, n. 11.
14 *Spartan*: from the city-state of Sparta, with a warlike reputation.

7 Landlord and tenant[1,2] 11 and 18 December 1841[3]

LANDLORD AND TENANT

"Look on this picture—and on this."

Nature had burst night's trammels, and the sun—
From the rich glowing portals of the East—
Had shed a flood of radiance o'er the plains.
The occident had sent it's zephyr forth
To pour the perfume of the mountain flower
In sweet libation to the infant day.
From every blushing petal trembling hung
A diamond dew-drop—like the glistening tear
That lingers in bright beauty's brilliant eye,
While her fair cheek is dimpled by a smile,
The earliest ray had woo'd me from my couch
To watch the rosy wing of morning flap
The murky shades in gaity away;
I stood upon a verdant hill, and gazed
On nature's chessboard which before me lay,
In varying beauty spread—the infant ear
Had burst its emerald shroud, and timidly
Shrunk from the balmy breeze's bland caress.
The meadow spread its carpet to the sun,
On which the brightest gems in Flora's[4] crown,
Like topas blushed—on the horizon's verge,
In far perspective azure mountains rose,
Bathing their peaks in ether—'rapt I stood,
And viewed the lovely scene—th' immortal mind
Expanded, and sought converse with the skies.
Acknowledging the goodness infinite,
I bowed before creation's GOD, and mine!

A hoary occupier of the soil
Approached the flower-crown'd hillock where I stood;
I marked his placid eye—the impetuous fire
Which burned there once was dimmed—and in its place
A calm and holy glow lit up its cheek.
Full seventy winter on his furrowed brow
Had spent their vehemence—yet smiling sat

Contentment there as lingers day's last beam,
In peaceful radiance on the rugged cliff.
His path lay near my stranding place—I turned,
And in my kindest accents bade—"good morning"—
The customary salutation passed—
The weather was our theme, from that anon
The smiling scene which lay before our eyes.
"See," said the patriarch, "where yon distant wreath
"Of sapphire smoke, upon the mountain air,
"Is borne sunward—where the sheltering trees
"Preclude alike the sunbeam and the blast.
"There is my home—within the selfsame shade
"The boyhood of my father's father passed;
"Beneath a towering lime which widely throws
"Its leaf-clad arms round, the good old man
"Resigned his breath—his son has also trod,
"Full twenty years ago, the darksome vale.
"The hoary scion of this mouldered stock,
"I, till the spot, where once its foliage bloomed;
"My daughters portioned off, a hardy son
"remains with me—the incense of whose prayer
"Ascends with mine to heaven's high throne, and calls
"Its richest blessings down upon the man
"Who gave us all—when upas blight fell,
"When whirlwinds premature have wildly swept
"Across earth's bosom, laying waste our fields
"With desolating power—meagre and chill
"Gaunt poverty has scowled upon our hearth;
"His smile benignant ever has dispelled
"The sable shades which gathered round my soul!
"When from life's tendril, like the blighted leaf,
"I trembling hang—in prayer my dying tongue
"Shall falter feebly forth 'God bless my Landlord.'"

II

The parting ray of the autumnal sun
Was slumbering on each "ivy-mantled" pile,
Which crowned in hoary grandeur every hill.
I neared my home—anticipation cast
The shroud of time aside—each playmate dear
Before me smiling stood, and breathed a welcome;

How sweet the thought—the kind, the warm embrace
Absorbed reflection—happy, happy youth!
Ideal time, when on utopian wing
Sweet fancy gaily soars on air ambrosial;
Alas! that stern reality should crush
Thy visionary towers.—I reached my home,
And eyes that once beamed kindly passed me by
Unheedingly—dark strife had raised her flag
Where kindred hearts had throbbed in unison.

One smiling morn, by inclination led,
I wandered forth reflecting as I went
On bygone days.—There is a peaceful spot
(Thought I,) where discord has not raised his brand;
I'll to't, and view fair happiness once more.
I climbed a hill, and from its mossy peak
I viewed the scene around—no smoky curl
Danced on the eddies of the atmosphere.
Onward I went towards the happy spot—
For so I deemed it still—no sound arose
To wake the sleeping echoes of the shade;
Each tree appeared to weep, as from the bough,
the leaflets seared and severed dropped to earth;
A sad foreboding filled my anxious mind,
When what I sought now burst upon my view!
Black, desolate and dreary—roofless walls
Upreared themselves, on which each passing breeze
Lavished a sigh—fixed to the spot I stood,
And traced the work of ruin's ruthless hand.

Upon a rugged stile a being sat;
He seemed inanimate—as if his mind
Abstracted from the earth, had wandered from
Its tenement, which waited its return.
His forehead pale was by a grisly hand
Intensely pressed.—I, wondering, asked the cause
Of all I saw.—He started at my voice,
And, like a reckless maniac answered—"THERE!"
"The darkest shroud is cast o'er all my hopes;
"THERE have I lived in happiness—and THERE
"My aged father heaved his dying sigh;
"I see his angry ghost indignant frown

"Upon his guilty son.—Oh! here I might
"Have spent a happy life, wer't not for ONE!
"Damn him, ye furies!—on the guilty thing
"Heap burning coals, and oh, ye vengeful skies
"Rain black perdition on his lonely grave!
"Oh! I could the darksome thoughts which now revolve
"Within my tortured mind, be quick enrobed
"In hottest flame!—and were my burning breast
"A thunder-cloud to roll the lightning on—
"In dire explosion, on the miscreant's head,
"I'd shower the vengeance of a ruined man!
"Curst be the hour he came with silver tongue,
"And Syren sounds[5] to woo me to my doom!
"To suit my taste a bauble first he dressed,
"And called it "Freedom"—God! I've found it false!
"False as the fruit that blooms in hell's abyss!
"He talked of pampered tyranny—he said
"I was a slave—and I, poor fool, believed.
"Mis'ries, 'till then unknown, sprung up before
"My jaundiced view—imaginary wrongs
"Lent fuel to the furnace of my brain,
"And viper-like, I turned and madly stung
"(Oh! base ingratitude,) the man that fed me.
"T'was done!—He cast the reptile from his breast—
"Deserted by the fiend who worked my woe—
"Dark desolation scowling o'er my fate,
"A wretched houseless wanderer I roam."

Carlow Sentinel, 11 and 18 November 1841, [3][6]
Typewritten transcript only

1 *Landlord and Tenant*: in his journal, Tyndall made several references to relationships between landlords and tenants in Ireland, particularly during the time of the emerging Great Famine, after the failure of the potato crop. Though he saw many of the (implicitly Catholic) tenants as dirty and indolent, he believed that the absentee landlords should shoulder their share of the load in relieving poverty and helping their tenants to work and survive. By implication, the happy tenant in this poem is Protestant and the wretched one Catholic.
2 Written under the pseudonym W. S. (Walter Snooks).
3 Tyndall was in Kinsale, working for the Irish Ordnance Survey.
4 *Flora's*: the Roman goddess of flowers and the Spring.
5 *Syren sounds*: the Sirens were creatures of Greek mythology who lured sailors to shipwreck.
6 For a commentary on this poem, see DeArce, McGing and McMillan (2013–14) 'Two Forgotten Poems by John Tyndall', though it has many transcription errors.

8 Lines sent with a forget me not[1] *early 1840s*

Fond memory's flower of azure dye
I send my fairest now to thee
Oh let it on thy bosom lie
An emblem of my love for thee

And if a glance should downward bend
And rest perchance upon that spot
That glance will prove affection's friend
Twill bring to mind "Forget me not"

RI MS JT/3/42/26

1 This poem is derived from an original by Mrs Opie, *The Oriental Herald and Journal of General Literature*, London: Richardson, 3 (1824): 539:

To the flower called, Forget Me Not!

Fond memory's flower of azure dye
Permit thy bard one boon to crave
When in death's narrow bed I lie,
Oh! bloom around my humble grave.

And if some tender faithful friend
Should, led by love, approach the spot,
And o'er thy flowers admiring bend,
Then say for me, Forget Me Not!

9 Acrostic (Christina Tidmarsh)[1] early August 1842[2]

Acrostic Cork Aug/42[3]

C an the storm tost seaman roam
H eedless thoughtless of his home
R ays from memory's brilliant star
I llumine his pathway from afar
S o dear girl I'll think of thee
T ost on life's tempestuous sea
I n my souls deep essence fraught
N ever canst thou be forgot
A s o'er thy cheek in bland caress
T rembling hangs each raven tress
I n thine eyes translucent light
D eeply, darkly, purely, bright
M id the halo of thy smile
A ll my cares I could beguile
R est fond thought,—for ever dwell
S tranded in thy silent cell
H ence I roam—sweet girl farewell

RI MS JT/8/2/1/11

1 Christina Tidmarsh was the sister of one of Tyndall's surveying colleagues, John Francis (Jack) Tidmarsh (1824–1906), and Tyndall seems to have had a soft spot for her.

2 Tyndall was in Cork working for the Irish Ordnance Survey. He sailed to Liverpool on 5 August.

3 This poem was written just as Tyndall sailed to England for the first time, to work on the English Survey, leaving Christina behind in Ireland.

10 To Ginty[1] October 1842[2]

Tho' grim disappointment his shadows may fling
        Oer the thoughts which like sunbeams once brightened my breast
As the angel of night with his ebony wing
        Sweeps the bright tints of eve from the beautiful west

Yet hope thro' the vista of time like a star
        To gild my existence lends many a beam
Its soul cleansing radiance it flings from afar
        To wake each gay ripple that laughs on life's stream

Then tune thy wild harp Bill to sadness no more
        Tho' sweet be the numbers & tender the strain
Let us hope for the hour when with ardent "encore"
        We'll revive our "discussions" in glory again

But fling (for thou canst) oer the musical string
        That hand which can waken its loveliest tone
May hope cosy hope round thy bosom still cling
        And happiness make every fibre its own

RI MS JT/8/2/1/11

1 William (Bill) Ginty (c.1820–66) worked with Tyndall on the Irish Ordnance Survey and later in England. Ginty shared lodgings with Tyndall until he was transferred to England on 20 May 1842.

2 In October 1842 Tyndall was based in Preston while Ginty was working elsewhere in northern England, particularly around Kirkby Lonsdale in Westmorland.

11 To Chadwick[1] 1 November 1842[2]

Dear Chadwick now the shaken sea
Uplifts its waves twixt you and me.
But say can such brief absence blight
The soul's affection once so bright.
Has dark oblivion swept thy breast,
As night the amber from the west
Must I believe I have no part
And fill no space in Chadwick's heart?
Is this the case? if so farewell
One dream on which I loved to dwell
One thought which o'er my senses stole
And wound its fibres round my soul—
Cherished alike on land and sea
That I possessed a friend in thee.

For other themes I must address
The muse, and now about our mess.
Among the things I mean to mention
It fairly claims the first attention.
Divide by 5 an even score
The quotient surely must be four.
This fits our numbers to a man
For Evans[3] lately joined the clan
Who thrice a day with nimble feet
Do wend their way to Butler Street.[4]
A cap they say in days of yore
The Lord of Moslem Turkey wore
Whose magic power could fulfil
Each wish the Sultan chose at will.
Oh that I had it! Chadwick dear
In thirty seconds you'd be here
Borne swifter than the rushing wind
Your wife and Lizzy[5] left behind.
Then might you at your leisure trace
The workings of each messman's face
As circling round the groaning table
They eat while ever they are able.

But as such caps are rather rare
('Thank god'! be Mrs Chadwick's prayer)
In words I must the life convey
Which quivers here from day to day
Behold us then each misty morn
Smitten at times by rain and storm
See us I say at half past six
As with our pale compeers we mix
The cheek all blue, the nose all red,
The thoughts all centred in the bed.
Whereas each stiff hand wields the pen
Its owner yearns to be again.
But time flows on—and hark the cry,
And mark the sparkle of each eye,
Which welcome loud & still the chime
That tinkles forth "tis breakfast time".
Mid rumble of confusions sweet
Each hungry draftsman seeks the street
Left face! and quick as you are able
Dash forward to our breakfast table.
Bill, George, & Phil[6] on coffee feast
While I, dissenting from their taste
Despise their fare and mix agog
My gentle cocoa in a mug.
It cheers my spirits, makes me fatter
Though my companions doubt the latter
And one there is who sweareth solus
We'd sooner breakfast on a bolus.
At dinner now behold the group
Breathing the fumes of gravy soup
Oh! for an angel's pen to trace
The varied twists of George's face
High in the air his mighty nose[7]
Its pleasure rests in sundry blows.
Their ponderous jaws the others ply
A dog's delight in every eye.
Till stuffed with flesh or tired of bone
They yield the fight and dinner's done.
At dinner tis my lot to serve
My office is to cut and carve
The sweat drops on his dewy brow

Attest what Tyndall suffers now.
'A small bit John' says George & Bill
"The merest morsel" echoes Phil.
Thus do I waste my precious life
Oh! happy thou who hast a wife!
Is there no maiden in the land
To snatch <u>me</u> from this glutton band.
To loose those feelings packed and pent
Like clouds within my firmament
To chase the fog with radiant eyes
And bid the sun in glory rise.

RI MS JT/8/2/1/14–15

1 John Chadwick, a surveying colleague of Tyndall, left the Irish Survey on 26 February 1842, probably because of the birth of his daughter, and settled in the town of Kinsale in County Cork, where he worked as a private surveyor.
2 Tyndall was in Preston, working for the English Ordnance Survey.
3 *Evans*: Phillip Deighton (Jim) Evans (c.1822–1906), a close surveying colleague of Tyndall.
4 *Butler Street*: Tyndall and others lodged at some time at 11 Butler Street, close to the railway and North Union Station in central Preston.
5 *Your wife and Lizzy*: Lizzy appears to be his daughter.
6 *Bill, George, & Phil*: Bill is possibly William Marquis (1820/1–95), and George and Phil probably George Latimer and Phillip Evans, all surveying colleagues based in Preston.
7 *mighty nose*: George Latimer's nose was an object of fun to Tyndall. See also poem 39.

12 Suggested on hearing High Mass in Saint Wilfred's Chapel[1,2] c.1843[3]

Hushed is the clangour of the vesper bell—
It's dying chime the breeze has borne away;
Around me now, no buzzing murmurs swell
While led by curiosity, I stray
Thro' Wilfred's holy fane—in white array
The fathers of the prostrate people stand,
Who deem the beamings of supernal day,
Or shades of Hades spread at their command
In glory or in gloom throughout the subject land![4]

And here bend youth and age, and here the tears
of pearly pureness, fill the dark fringed eyes
Of lovely penitents, while ghostly fears
Sweep from their downy cheeks the vermeil dyes—
The roseate tints which slumbered there—and sighs
From iron hearts are sent, as haply lours
The frown of Rome—like barbs and bolts it flies,
Piercing the soul, and crushing all its powers—
Before her mystic shrines th' immortal essence cowers!

See yonder time-worn soldier where he kneels,
With tattooed brow—with bosom scorched and scarred!
Can fearless spirits feel as how he feels?
Can this be he who erst the battle dared;
When sanguinary files tumultuous jarred,
With life compressed and challenge-flashing eye,
He sought the cloud of conflict helmet-starred,
He sunk—yet rose above the din his cry—
Untrammelled—unsubdued—presage of victory!

He quails!—anon an Orphean spell combined
With all the shadowy grandeurs that arise
From canvass and from candles, grasp his mind—
Lifting imagination to the skies—
They generate a feeling which defies
The manacles of reason, as it soars
Beyond the world, in speechless extacies,

To realms where Francis and Stylites pour
The ceaseless tide of praise and Heaven's bright Queen adores!

Oh! there's a witchery in that thrilling peal—
That requiem of common sense—which turns
The soul to high-wrought phrenzy—even I feel
Its mighty influence—tho' my spirit spurns
Rome's scarlet draperies,—her unctions,—wens
Cowls,—curses,—, and chimeras—dark and dire
That dense azotic cloud within which burns,
In lurid vigour superstitious fire;
But where alas! the beams of intellect expire!

Wat Ripton Snooks

Preston Lancashire

RI MS JT/8/2/1/16–17

1 St Wilfred's is a Catholic Church in Chapel Street, Preston, close to the railway station and to Fishergate. During his time in Preston, Tyndall attended churches and chapels of several denominations, including Anglican and Methodist. For a discussion of Tyndall's early religious development see Cantor 2015.
2 Written under the pseudonym Wat Ripton Snooks.
3 Tyndall once recalled in his journal hearing Mass in this church on 25 December 1842 (25 December 1843, RI MS JT/2/13a/9). This poem may have been written shortly afterwards, when Tyndall was in Preston.
4 The original first verse reads as follows:

The bells had ceased and solemnly subdued
Was all the bustle of the noisy throng,
When in Saint Wilfred's fane I stood and viewed
The prostrate ranks which stretched the aisles along,
And heard the bosom thrilling choral song
Which bathed in floods of melody the span
Of the high dome—as swelled aloft among
The towering columns—glowing as it ran
From soul to kindred soul the rapturous paean!

13 On leaving Westmorland[1] January 1843[2]

Farewell to the land of the crag and the cloud,
Which mantles each mountain, where fearfully loud,
The wild tempest revels, and branchless and bare,
Lays the prince of the hills, erst majestic and fair.
Farewell to the fells where the faint bleating notes
Are oft flung to the breeze by the perishing goats.
The tear-drops fall quickly while from you I fly;
Ye crags, and ye thunder-rent caverns, good bye!

Farewell ye dark summits, where fancy has wrought
Her loveliest visions—ye temples of thought,
Where my bosom untramelled has swelled with delight,
As the Windermere[3] beauties have burst on my sight;
Where my soul in her essence exultingly soared,
Or the God of creation in meekness adored.
But the visions have faded and melted the spell,
Ye haunts of sublimity's genius, farewell!

By Heaven! I love you—the feelings which bind
Us are strong as o'er bound things material with mind;
But my heart!—shall I utter the working that's there?
Shall my stanza be marred by the clink of despair?
As autumn complains of the blight of the spring,
Of the mildews which summer has shook from her wing;
Thus, thus, will I warble my woe-begone tale,
Till the chimneys of Liverpool[4] echo my wail.

Oh! why has just heaven permitted the snare?
Or why wert *thou* made so surpassingly fair?
Were the soft downy cheek and the roseate smile
Bestowed thee to strengthen each hope-crushing wile?
Can I ever forget the perfection of bliss,
Which pervaded my soul when my first burning kiss
Was with ardour impressed on thy beautiful cheek,
And my eyes volumed forth what my tongue could not speak.

Has the ruby a glow?—round thy sweet lips it shone:
Has a Nainde a grace?—it was surely thine own:
Has the rosebud a fragrance?—the tulip a hue?

Has an angel a glory?—it beamed around you:
When it twinkles in beauty o'er Italy's skies,
Has the eve-star a ray?—oh! it dwelt in thine eyes.
With a Persian's high favour, when called to adore,
I gazed on thee—loved thee—what could I do more?

Oh! talk to me not of the gay vernal bloom,
Of the jessamine's dyes, or the lily's perfume;
Can the joyance of spring to the mouldering heart,
Hope's promises bring, or hope's soothings impart?
Ah! no—in the depths of Cimmerian night,[5]
Lie buried my prospects, erst gloriously bright:
My Mary is false! oh! the thought is a hell;
Ye records of trampled affection—FAREWELL.

Preston Chronicle, 28 January 1843, [4]
Typewritten transcript only

1 Signed 'W. Ginty', this poem is a prank by Tyndall, narrating Ginty's discovery of his 'false' Mary. He even sent a copy anonymously to her, following which there was a scene amid some concern that her family might see it (James Sinnett to John Tyndall, 2 February 1843, RI MS JT/1/TYP/11/3863, letter 0184 in TC1), especially since Mary's engagement to someone else had just been announced (William Ginty to John Tyndall, 31 January 1843, RI MS JT/1/TYP/11/3591, letter 183 in TC1). Ginty found the affair highly amusing. Mary Edwards (b. c.1822) lived with her uncle and aunt in Kirkby Lonsdale and, despite having a putative romance with William Ginty, married William Henry Owen, an Irish solicitor, in June 1843.
2 Tyndall was in Preston, working for the English Ordnance Survey.
3 *Windermere*: the largest lake in the Lake District, in northern England.
4 At this date Ginty (but not Tyndall) was living in Liverpool.
5 *Cimmerian night*: in Greek mythology, the Cimmerians lived in perpetual mist and darkness near the land of the dead.

14 An Hibernian's Song. To—.[1,2] 20 May 1843[3]

Oh! my beautiful queen its yourself that is neat,
As fair as the flower that blooms in the grove,
When your beautiful form you bend o'er the street,
By the holy Saint Hospice[4]—I'm smothered in love!

Now listen, my dear, if you treat with disdain,
The tears of affection which stand in my eye,
Or carelessly laugh at my sowl-sinking pain,
By the holy Saint Hospice—my angel I'll die!

My heart how it flutters—oh! could I but tell
How I think of you, dearest, by day and by night,
When the snores of the million in melody swell
I dream that I clasp you in furious delight!

From the mountains of Erin[5] I've brought you a heart
As big as a steam coach!—I solemnly swear!
Oh! my admirable jewel—my princess impart
A beautiful kiss for to cheer its despair!

Oh! had I the gifts which for sartin belong
To the great Dan O'Connell,[6] with blarney galore,
Like a hero I'd swear at the end of my song,
By the pow-dhers of turf![7]—its yourself I adore!

Preston Chronicle, 20 May 1843, [4]
Typewritten transcript only

1 The object of Tyndall's affection (Tyndall being the 'Hibernian', or Irishman) in this poem is not clear.
2 Signed Wat Ripton: one of Tyndall's nom de plumes.
3 Tyndall was in Preston, working for the English Ordnance Survey.
4 *Saint Hospice*: possibly a reference to the reclusive French saint of the sixth century.
5 *Erin*: romantic name for Ireland.
6 *Dan O'Connell*: see poem 3, n. 6.
7 *By the pow-dhers of turf*: an Irish imprecation.

15 Pour mon cher Jack[1] 1 July 1843[2]

Dear Jack, ere the pennant above thee is streaming,
A meteor tracing its path thro the sky—
While Remembrance o'er pleasures departing is dreaming,
I raise my blunt steel-nib to wish thee Good Bye![3]
And shall I appeal to the empty illusion,
That floats o'er Parnassus, and raise with the throng,
The incense of prayer for the fancied infusion
Of light from the muse to embellish my song?
Away with the mock'ry—the language of feeling
Is fairest disrobed of the tinsel of art;
Its musical tomes a deep pathos revealing
Bear on them the fair, sunny stamp of the heart!
Oh! peaceful and soft my dear Jack be thy pillow,
Encircled by thoughts of the fair native shore;
As riding secure o'er the foam crested billow,
Thou dreamest of Friendship and Tyndall once more!
How I think on the nights we have nestled together!
When the voice of 'discussion' waxed warm and shrill—
They are vanished and flown like a wind-borne feather,
Yet deeply doe Memory cherish them still!
And oh! when he roams by the brink of the ocean
Which laves that far shore with its wavelets of blue—
When his heart is alive to each tender emotion,
I feel that my Tidmarsh will think of them too!
And with them remember the green sunny mountains
Of Erin,[4] which lift their proud summits on high;
Forget not her vales, nor her flowers, nor her fountains
Where the bright smile of Boyhood first gleamed in thine eye!
There are bosoms which love thee, whose full tide of sorrow
Is fanned as it flows by a thousand fond fears;
There are bright eyes and lovely which scarcely can borrow
From Hope a glad sunbeam to dry up their tears!
Yet, onward my Boy! may the balm-wafting pinion
Of unalloyed happiness wave o'er thy breast;
When far, far away from the Sappers[5] dominion
Your thoughts wander back to 'your own darling West'![6]
May the God of your fathers protect you in danger
While your course o'er the dark-rolling surges you steer
Till you press the bright strand of the Ishmaelite stranger,

And the warm tones of welcome strike sweet on thine ear!
And now ere the pennant above thee is streaming,
A meteor tracing its path thro' the sky—
While Remembrance o'er pleasures departed is dreaming
Last chime of my song, Jack—God Bless you—Good Bye!

RI MS JT/1/11/3873[7]
Typewritten transcript only

1 This poem was sent in a letter to John (Jack) Tidmarsh. See also poem 9, n. 1.
2 On this date, Tyndall, based in Preston, was about to leave on a break of a fortnight to the nearby village of Goosnargh, where he arrived on 3 July.
3 It appears from the poem that Tidmarsh was returning to Ireland, perhaps to see his family.
4 *Erin*: romantic name for Ireland.
5 *Sappers*: a reference to working under the Royal Engineers on the Ordnance Survey.
6 *'your own darling West'!*: Tidmarsh was brought up in Cork, in the south-west of Ireland.
7 See also John Tyndall to John Tidmarsh, 1 July 1843 (letter 214, TC1).

16 [Such bliss] 4 July 1843[1]

Such bliss for which my spirit sighs
Thou[2] canst give, for Oh! it lies
Hid within thy lovely eyes.
Breathes a stranger now his vow
As thy glance is round him dancing
Rife with rapture—by that brow
Too divine and too enchanting
Oft I've sworn since I met thee
Never, never to forget thee
Eastern breezes softly sighing
Lingering o'er the sunny lees
Zephyrs whispering thro' the trees
All is music to mine ear
But thy voice is far more dear.

RI MS JT/2/13a/v
Typewritten transcript only

1 Written at Goosnargh, a village close to Preston, where Tyndall had arrived on 3 July.
2 *Thou*: while in Goosnargh, Tyndall generated a passion for Elizabeth (Lizzy) Barton, youngest daughter of the landlord of the General Elliott pub. However, this poem may refer to an unknown young lady in Preston, as Tyndall had only arrived in Goosnargh the previous day.

17 [The day is gone] 12 July 1843[1]

The day is gone, no golden beam
Now smiles upon the fair hill side,
And cheerless flows the darkling stream
By weeping flowers which fringe its side.
The day is gone, and darkness flings
Her mantle over crag and dell
Its caroll now no warbler sings,
Amid the brakes of Berkenfell:[2]
But higher notes convulsive rise,
The booming of the angry sea,
The thrilling war songs of the skies
Now dwells in wildering melody.
There's something lofty in the feeling,
That swathes my soul with burning glow,
Too grand, too glorious for revealing,
Too high to grovel here below:
When fancy spreads her daring plume,
And curbless wings amid the gloom,
Her welkin sweeping flight to rise,
And mingle with her native skies!
Past hours into existence start,
And scenes long lived round my heart:
yes, burning thro' the gloom afar
Is seen the golden glowing star
of memory, whose brilliant rays
sheds glory over bygone days.
The days when boyhoods reckless joy
Rung forth unmingled with alloy;
When generosity and truth
Shone frontlets on the brow of youth;
When with a swimmers dauntless pride,
I skimmed the barrows[3] placed tide.
Oh! these give memory a zest,
And sheds a halo round my breast.
The 'decent church' still topples there,[4]
Where first my childhood lisped a prayer;
While round are strewn the graven stones,
Chill records of the mouldering bones
Which lie beneath, as sadly waves

The rank grass o'er the lonely graves.
Ah! how I loved when smiling even
Blushed beauteous in the western heaven;
As rose the merle's[5] farewell note,
To clamber up the lofty mote,[6]
And from the fairy legioned mound,
To view the lovely scene around.
The ripple of the brooklet near[7]
Struck sweetly soothing on mine ear;
And rich in beauties varied dies,
The groves of Burgage[8] blessed my eyes.
Beyond, amid the stately trees,
Where softly crept the evening breeze,
Which as it sighed o'er lawn and bower,
Kissed perfume from each drooping flower,
'The Lodges'[9] appeared—beneath me rolled
The gentle barrow tinged with gold
How calmly would the sunbeams smile
Upon the castle's hory pile:[10]
Not always thus[11]—the sabres flash
Glanced lightning there—the commons crash
Rung thunder o'er the startled flood,
And stained its chrystal waves with blood!
But peaceful is his war seared brow
And silent are his thunders now:
The pall of centuries is spread
In gloom oer many crested head,
Where proudly waved the nodding plume,
Amid the battles deepest gloom:
They're gone—and now the ivy clings,
And many a songster safely sings,
Where erst the clarion blasted far
The thrilling notes of blood and war!
Oh! how would thoughts like these unbind
The trammels from my embryon mind:
Aroused as by a glowing beam,
The young chrysalis ceased to dream
Assumed the wing and stretched its flight
Thro' scenes by fancy rendered bright.
'Twas then I ventured first to fling
My hand across the trembling string;

Tho' wild and broken was its tone,
I loved it, for it was my own,
Oft would my straggling bosom long
To wreak its thoughts on nobler song.
Hail! happy hours e'en now ye shine,
The brightest gems in memorys chime
Hail! blissful scenes, between us swell
The crested wave and towering fell
And now perchance the surging gale
Sweeps oer you wild with frenzied wail.
Hark how it sobs—its murderous breath
Now haply strews the shore with death.
The embers of the wasted fire,
Now quickly one by one expire,
A waning lamp in
Flings oer my page its dying blaze;
Admonished by the midnight chime
My wary pen I now resign
My couch to seek while wild and high,
The tempest sings my lullaby
(finis)

RI MS JT 8/2/1/20–1[12]
Typewritten transcript only

1 This is one of three poems Tyndall wrote on the same day in Goosnargh. See also poems 18 and 19.
2 *Berkenfell*: this appears to be an imaginary mountain, with a name resonant of the north of England. It is first mentioned in a poem in a letter from William Ginty to Tyndall, 11 November 1842. See letter 0174, n. 23, TC1.
3 *barrows*: the River Barrow, which flows through Leighlinbridge.
4 *The 'decent church' still topples there*: probably a reference to either the medieval Wells Church in Leighlinbridge, where Tyndall's uncle Caleb was a church warden, or St Laserian's Cathedral in Old Leighlin, where Tyndall's father would be buried in the family plot in 1847. A 'decent

church' is presumably a Protestant one, and may relate to directives on ecclesiastical furniture in the English Church Canons such as 'A decent Communion-table in every Church' (Canon LXXXII) (letter 0217, n. 9, TC1).

5 *merle*: a blackbird.

6 *lofty mote*: the Moat of Ballyknockan, the only remaining part of the Dinn Righ, the ancient seat of the Kings of Carlow, south of Leighlinbridge near the west bank of the River Barrow (letter 0146, n. 17, TC1).

7 *the brooklet near*: presumably Maudlin stream, a tributary of the Barrow (letter 0146, n. 18, TC1).

8 *Burgage*: a parish in County Carlow.

9 *'The Lodges'*: possibly Burgage House, seat of the Vigors family (letter 0217, n. 14, TC1).

10 *the castle's hory pile*: the remains of Carlow Castle, a Norman structure built between 1207 and 1213 (letter 0217, n. 17, TC1).

11 *Not always thus*: Carlow Castle was besieged in 1495 amid the repercussions of a plot to seize the English crown, and again during the Confederate Wars of 1641–2, when more than 400 Anglo-Irish Protestants were trapped by Catholic Confederate forces and starved for three months. It was also besieged by Oliver Cromwell's New Model Army in 1650 (letter 0217, n. 18, TC1).

12 See also John Tyndall to Editor of *The Carlow Sentinel*, 12 July 1843 (letter 217, TC1). The letter was not published. Annotations to this poem are derived from this letter.

18 [The aerial phantazies of youth] 12 July 1843[1]

The aerial phantazies of youth
Robed in their own bright loveliness—
The visions clothed with seeming truth
Now melted into nothingness!—
Aye, all are vanished—yet not so
Behind the evanescent throng
There linger still a holy glow—
A beam which 'gilds thy every song'!
Whence comes it?—does the scented gale
From distant Kirkby[2] bear the prize?
Or does the heav'nly brightness dwell
In 'lovely Mary's'[3] diamond eyes?—
Ah! no—it shines upon the breast
Of every billow wild and high
Which rears aloft its foamy crest,
Rebellious to the darkened sky—
It smiles, where ripples gently lave
Each barque that spreads her snowy sail
On every rock—on every wave
Between 'New Babel'[4] and Kinsale!
Yes—there its nucleus dwells, to bless
Thy morning thought—thy midnight sigh
There clusters too 'the raven tress'
There radiates the lustrous eye—
The clouds of care may gloom and lour
In darkling masses round thy breast,
There is a ray of magic power—
As glorious sunbeam from the West!
Which calls to life thy buried love—
The 'cup of sweets' without alloy
And like a spirit from above
Gives vigour to the pulse of joy!—
*Oh! there are ideas which dart—
Like meteors thro' the midnight air
A gleam of glory thro' the heart
Where waved the banner of despair!
Visions of bliss untasted roll
Before the visionary ken—
Destroy the canker of the soul

And bid the mourner smile again.
I know I touch a speaking string—
A string which quivers in thy core
And sounds responsive while I sing
Of days which shall return no more—
of whom? oh! God of poesy
My log should smoke and blaze and flame
And consecrations from on high
should sparkle round her sacred name!
of whom?—of Ellen[5]—oh! I find
My swelling bosom's deep devotion
Unutterable—while my mind
Is crushed by mountains of emotion!
Not so with you—you grasp the lyre
And shake from it the dust of slumber
From her you catch the heavenly fire
And unholy wake the burning number!
I love to con the glowing line
Where Ginty's restless spirit revels
And flings with fervours quite sublime
The fury of a dozen devils!—
I love to ponder o'er the lay
Where Ginty's muse does gentler duty
To wing his spirit quite away
Before the shrine of 'Mary's' beauty
But oh! a deeper—holier spell
Like music thro' the moonbeams streaming
Is riven thro' the fervid swell
And from the leader one is gleaming
When thoughts of lovely Ellen raise
The murmurs of this melting stream
And all 'the lights of other days'
Around thy stanza smiles again!
Farewell thou bright ideal ray—
Which lent to life its happiest hue—
Thou gleam of heaven's own halcyon day
Angelic hope—adieu!—adieu!—
oh give to him thy sunny smile—
I claim it not—that thought is flown
Upon my harp I lean the while
Its last sad twinkle dies—tis gone!!

*'oh! there are looks & tones which dart
An instant sunshine thro the heart
Byron[6]

RI MS JT 8/2/1/24–5[7]

1 This is one of three poems Tyndall wrote on the same day in Goosnargh. See also poems 17 and 19.
2 *Kirkby*: near Liverpool, where William Ginty was based.
3 *'lovely Mary's'*: Mary Edwards. See poem 12.
4 *'New Babel'*: Liverpool. See William Ginty to John Tyndall, 29 May 1842 (letter 144 in TC1).
5 *Ellen*: Ellen from Kinsale, possibly Ellen Wall, of 'the raven plume'.
6 In fact the lines are from Thomas Moore's *Lalla Rookh: An Oriental Romance* (1817) IV.i.685–6. He used them also in poem 28.
7 This poem is included in a letter from John Tyndall to William Ginty, 12 July 1843 (letter 218, TC1). An extensive draft of this poem also exists: RI MS JT/8/2/1/29–30.

19 Acrostic (Elizabeth Barton)[1] 12 July 1843[2]

Acrostic

E astern breezes softly sighing,
L ingering oer the sunny seas,
I n their own free transport flying,
Z ephyrs whispering thro' the trees—
A ll is music to mine ear,
B ut thy voice is doubly dear,
E very blessing that I prize,
T hou canst give, for oh! it lies
H id within thy lovely eyes!

B end thine ear to this my vow
A s thy glance is round me dancing,
R ife with rapture—by that brow
T oo divine, and too enchanting!
O h! by yon bright heaven above me,
N ever can I cease to love thee!

JTyndall

Written at Goosnargh
July 12th 1843 {Alas poor Goosnargh!}

RI MS JT/8/2/1/19

1 Elizabeth (Lizzy) Barton was the youngest daughter of the landlord of the General Elliot pub in Goosnargh, for whom Tyndall had an attraction, in competition with Billy Marquis.

2 This is one of three poems Tyndall wrote on the same day in Goosnargh. See also poems 17 and 18.

20 Acrostic (Miss Hebdon)[1] July 1843[2]

M orn smiles in loveliness on many a flower,
I n whose bright petals live the rainbows dyes,
S preading its perfume round the dew-dropped bower,
S weet tribute to the zephyr as it sighs.

H ow passing pure is evenings radiant star,
E ther its azure bed and tranquil home;
B right, beautiful, it beams from heaven afar,
D impling with lustre the cerulean dome.
O h! both are fair—but in thee both combine,
N ow grace that cheek, and light those eyes of thine.

RI MS JT/8/2/1/19

1 Miss Hebdon: not identified. The Hebdon family lived in Preston. See John Hebdon to Tyndall, 15 December 1843, letter 0279, TC2. This is possibly John Henry Hebdon (1822–?) who appeared on the 1851 census of Preston along with his wife Alice Hebdon (1824–83); his occupation was listed as 'Banker's clerk'.

2 Tyndall was in Preston, working for the English Ordnance Survey.

21 To N—T[1] July 1843[2]

From the green hills of Erin[3] I've plucked the wild rose,
  So fresh and so fragrant as washed by the dew,
Like a gem on the landscape each blossom arose,
  And gave to the sunbeam its odour and hue!

Like the rose of my country, sweet girl thou art fair,
  I think of its beauty while gazing on thee;
Could I cull the first floweret of Englands parterre
  To place on my bosom—there, there, shouldst thou be!

JTyndall

For Miss H[s] album[4]
July 1843

RI MS JT/8/2/1/19

1 *N—T*: not identified.
2 Tyndall was in Preston, working for the English Ordnance Survey.
3 *Erin*: romantic name for Ireland.
4 *Miss H[s] album*: this acrostic is written below poem 20, to Miss Hebdon.

22 [Acrostic (Jane)][1] *1840s*

J. oyous and bright is the glance of the morn
A. s it flings its deep radiance o'er eastern skies
N. or dimmer the hues which thy fair cheek adorn
E. ach dark beaming lay of thy beautiful eyes

W. aft her ye breezes my tale of devotion
I. n your soft music oh! murmur it well
L. ong shall I think of thee, love with emotion
D. eep in my heart shall thy idea dwell
G. one is my happiness—sweet one <u>farewell</u>

In every fancy ev'n now I can trace
Never shall time from my[2]

RI MS JT/8/2/1/20

1 Jane: not identified
2 The rest of this acrostic is missing. At the top, probably written by Louisa Tyndall in 1902 is: 'There was a second scrap of paper with continuation of this Acrostic L Mar02?'.

23 [More musical than twenty dozen rills] *1840s*

More musical than twenty dozen rills
Thy voice my charmer [feels me pace][1] thy hills
With lips [more sweet than lovely sand] jars
of jam; and eyes that part all the stars.
My truest one I hear them & I swear
Though I am <u>here</u> & thou my angel <u>there</u>
I'd crush all space to nothing to seek
Thy form [unparagoned] on [friendly] peak
My lovely one my fair, my dulcet duet
How could your [eyes] muster up the [planete]
To scale that crag a maiden sweet beware
It is a [supping] & an eager air
[Ten] Turkish baths [1 word illeg] thy lungs of phlegm
And those [unparagoned] [only say what of them]
From [blood with flame], & [waking with their past]
Thy [1 word illeg] all [1 word illeg] [tempest] [1 word illeg]
The undulations of thy snowy hair
Turned to a meteor in the mountain air
Come down my pet forsake that crag unblest
And lay thy little cheek upon this head.
Let them like arms thy snowy neck entwine
[Darling] I'll press them Oh my Valentine

RI MS JT/8/2/1/21

1 The handwriting in this poem is particularly bad.

24 [The star that gems life's morning sky] *1840s?*

The star that gems life's morning sky
Smiles sweetly on thee now
And flowers around thy pathway lie
And roses crown thy brow

Thy head was on my shoulder leaning
Thy hand in mine was gently prest;
Thine eyes so soft and full of meaning;
were bent on me and I was blest.

No word was spoken, all was feeling.
The silent transport of the heart.
The tear that o'er thy cheek was stealing
Told what words could ne'er impart.

And could this be but mine illusion?
Could fancy all so real seem?
Here fancy's scenes are wild confusion,
And can it be I did but dream?

I'm sure I felt thy forehead pressing,
Thy rosy breath stole o'er my cheeks
I'm sure I saw those eyes confessing
What the tongue could never speak.

Ah! No, t'is gone, t'is gone, and never
Mine such waking bliss can be;
Oh, I would sleep, would sleep for ever,
Could I thus but dream of thee!

Never forget our loves, but always cling
To the fixed hope that there will be a time
When we can meet unfettered and be blest
With the full happiness of certain love.

When thou art near,
    The sweetest joys still sweeter seem,
The brightest hopes more bright appear,
    And life is all one happy dream,
When thou art near.

RI MS JT/8/2/1/22

25 [We must part a while] *1840s*

We must part a while
A few short months—though short, they must be long
Without thy dear society; but yet
We must endure it and our love will be
The fonder after parting—it will grow
Intenser in our absence, and again
Burn with a tender glow when I return
Fear not; this is my last resolve, and this
My parting letter.

RI MS JT/8/2/1/23

26 [Oh Mary pon my soul][1] *1840s*

Oh Mary pon my soul my love
I love you very dear
The [1 word illeg] [hour] now rolls my love
& yet you are not here—
Amid the far blue ether love
My thoughts in welness roam
Can lovely Mary faithless prove
Oh! Why am I alone?—
When last I pressed your cheek my love
& trembled in your eye
The world was fast asleep my love
And full of stars the sky
You said you'd meet me here my love
When I my vigil keep
& while I think you false my love
I blow my nose and weep

Then come oh! come my only love
& cheer this poets heart
Oh Mary still the window sill
Is warmer than thou art
The morn is bright & cloudless love
& yet thou art not here
With diamond eyes my soaring dove
Appear appear appear!

RI MS JT/8/2/1/24

1 Mary is not identified.

27 [A desolate forlorn swain] *1840s?*

A desolate forlorn swain
Who loves and soothly loves in vain
Now pours his tide of griefs and fears
A weary girl whose bosom bright
Into a hundred poets ears
Has often bounded with delight
When Ellen's[1] radiant smiles impressed
A blissful image on my breast
Evn now the waves and mountains rise
Their towering summits to the skies
Between the [1 word illeg] still appears
Her dulcet accents bless my ears
Een now as memory cheers the gloom
I see afar her raven plume
Unfold each glossy trembling tress
Her snowy bosom to caress
Ye shadows of Egyptian night
Oh quench, for ever quench the light
Which busy recollection flings
Around my minds imaginings
Oh! thou oblivious Lethe roll
Thy cheerless billows o'er my soul
And wash the images away
The germs of my [brains] decay

Vain prayer – each flowret blooming fair
And waving in the summer air
Reminds me where in beauty blows
A fairer flower, a lovelier rose.
And now when water sheds its blight
On leaflet green and petal bright.
When oer the fields bleak Fevrier throws
Her dazzling counterpane of snows
When resting in its cavern deep
Each withering thought had courted sleep
Why wake them from their soft repose
Why rouse again my burning throes

For this oh! Ginty[2] – on thy head
I shower my imprecation dread
Around thy couch for ever dwell
The highest harmony of hell
May fury stamp in living flame
A blustery devil on thy fame
At last may hell's hot river roll
Its burning bellows oer thy soul

I pause—methinks my angry ban
Quite unbefitting of a man
The impulse of a flashing thought.
The sense of feelings over-wrought
But now I see—oh! jealous kind
The latent workings of thy mind
I cursed thee reckless of the Spring
Which moved thy muse and shook thy string
Where "Ellen's" memory's treasure hung
In trembling accent, on thy tongue
Oh! pity soft that in my breast
Has ever been a welcome guest
In tender accents let me pour
My vast—my overwhelming store
Of sympathy for Ginty's fears
His moving moans and midnight tears
Did you pour chilly valentine
With Ginty's [wonted] sparkle shine
Where was the poets fervour fled
Like Autumn leaflets seared and dead
The music of his song was hushed
His spirits noble phrenzy crushed
And cold and flat the raylet lay
That winged to Fishergate[3] its way.

RI MS JT/8/2/1/27–8

1 *Ellen's*: see poem 18, n. 5.
2 *Ginty*: William Ginty, see poem 10, n. 1. Ellen 'of the raven plume', from Kinsale, features in many letters and poems between them.
3 *Fishergate*: a street in Preston, near the railway station, where several of the surveyors appear to have lodged.

28 [Dont you remember love][1] *1840s*

Dont you remember love, one happy night
You granted me a little crumb of bread
Slipped thro the mystic ring which circled bright
Your taper finger—underneath my head
I placed the precious fragment—then I slept
And Fancy, wafted to the land of dreams
Through bright arcades with zephyrs softly crept
Oh! listen—pencilled with supernal beams
Before my ravished eye the future brightly gleams

Methought I wandered by a lovely river
Fringed with a thousand shrubs of various hue
O'er whose clear face the chestnut leaves did quiver
And flowrets bloomed as beautiful as you
It seemed a spirit gliding thro' the breast
of a signal vale—the hills on either side
And robes of waving foliage bravely dressed
Rose to the noonday sun in sylvan pride
Who from his high abode the tears of morn had dried

'It is not good for man to be alone'
Is Heaven's own dictum—Fancy thought so too
Mayhap she had no power of her own
But as in duty bound the curtain drew
Which veiled my destiny, so let that lie
Till some more subtle mind uncoil the charm
But while I wandered 'neath that sunny sky
The lord preserve my sinful soul from harm
A maiden bright as love clung gently to my arm

Her head was clothed with ringlets of rich brown
Which fell in clouds upon her snowy shoulder
Her Queenly brow was made to grace a crown
Her tinted cheek to ravish each beholder
Her eyes! By heaven her eyes! Oh who can tell
The latter vied in whiteness with the gown
of muslinet that softly did enfold her
Her brow was slightly arched her forehead fair
Her cheek a pure carnation lips clear red

As if the blood of roses trickled there
And roses breath a double fragrance shed
Around them as they slumbered on their pearly bed

And now I have disposed of many a grace
Possessed by this fair being—features dyes
And charms which lent enchantment to her face
But I have omitted mention of her eyes
Her eyes resembled what?—oh could I dare
To dig the brightest diamond from its mine
And say her eye, deep lustre dwellith there
Twere false

Those gems of heaven resembled what? oh I have
The question for I cannot tell many
The depth of witchery which slumbers there

Her head was clothed with ringlets of rich brown
Which fell in clouds upon her snowy shoulder
The latter vied in whiteness with the gown
Of muslinet, which softly did enfold her
Her brow was slightly curved, her forehead fair
Her cheek a light carnation, lips clear red
As if the blood of roses trickled there
And rose's breath a treble perfume shed
Around them as they slumbered on their pearly bed!

And now I have disposed of many a grace
Possessed by this fair being—features dyes
And charms that lent enchantment to her face
A dim hiatus still exists—her eyes!
What of them? Thirsa if I dare
Where shall I find their likeness—in the star
That gems yon heaven—or in the midnight hue
Her eyes! I no other subject shall [without]
Upon this stanza
One place alone on earth their equals beam
I'll lead thee gently where thou mayest see
Their archetypes—bend oer thy glassy stream
Behold them shining there as bright as in my dreams

Once I remember Thirsa to have seen
Three graces, from the chisel of Canova
And read with pleasure of a certain Queen
Belovéd by Gonzales de Cordova

Oh! give me a lay that sparkles bright
with the gems of the radiant soul
A song for my Thirsa ever bright
As I quaff the generous bowl
Let it shine with the hue which [trickles] dark
The spirits hidden spring
From the fount of truth let the [1 word illeg] leap[2]

And now I have disposed of many a grace
Possessed by this fair being, features dyes
And charms that lend enchantment to her face
A dim hiatus still exists—her eyes!
Where shall I find their likeness? Come with me
One place alone on earth their equals beam
Nay frown not Thirsa thou shalt see
Their bright reflection & confess the same

Her eyes! Oh lovely Thirsa who can tell
The depth of witchery, which slumbered in them there
Now soft as sunset their full glances fell
Anon half closed with such a [dreaming] air.
They murdered thro their fringes and yet again
they sparkled like a brilliant in a mine
To gaze upon thy looking glass & then
But words are vain & feeble is my pen
to paint their power
Oh suck not all their beauty from my pen
With most enchanting wickedness and then
But why continue

RI MS JT/8/2/1/31–2

1 Parts of this poem also appear in drafts of 'With cloudy head' (poem 29). The manuscript shows extensive working, with about 50 alterations. The repetitions have been left as they were written.

2 This stanza is written across the page.

29 [With cloudy head][1] *1840s*

With cloudy head and discontented breast
As I sat basking in the setting sun
And wishing time defunct—an unbid guest
Made supper on my shin—and oft he'd run
In frolick gambols o'er the downy plains
Anon he'd fix his little fangs in me
And quaff a bounteous potion from my veins
And twitch my <u>cutis</u> most unpleasantly
I turned my stocking down—behold! It was a flea
I clutched him but he bounded from my thumb
and like a bloodhound I pursued
Determined to revenge upon his limb
The insult offered to my flesh and blood
Ho, for the merry chase!—tis sweet to see
The stretching pack on mountainside or level
And I can not my Hark forward on the flea
For in the jaws of death he seemed to revel
Threw somersets and galloped like the devil!

I lost my game, though many a deadly poke
I made, and oft was certain of my prize
But still the miscreant nullified my stroke
And pricked his tail & seemed to blast my eyes
My wrath grew high, but he continued cool
My blows fell thick, but he evaded all
And frisking 'neath the shadow of a stool
he vanished from my view and 'scaped my thrall
the varlet! Had I caught him, faith he'd squall!

'Labour is worship' so some sage has said
And surely it preserves from many an evil
And though it may not lift to Heaven the head
It keeps the heart from wandering to the devil[2]
Thus while this tiny beast my thoughts engaged
I felt the care clouds from my brain disperse
And though when blinked I was the least enraged
It worked for good & now in [numbers terse]
And lightened heart give his pranks a place in here
With happy heart my flea's renown in verse!

RI MS JT/8/2/1/33–5

1 This poem is sufficiently distinct from other drafts to stand separately, and this is the second, neater version, on f. 34. The rest, on f. 35, overlaps substantially with drafts of 'Dont you remember love' (poem 28).

2 Tyndall sent the four lines ending here, presumably a reference to Thomas Carlyle, to his cousin Hector Tyndale on 27 July 1855 (RI MS JT/1/T/1443; RI MS JT/1/TYP/1604–9).

30 To Elizabeth[1] *1840s*

Sweet sleep has sealed the weary eyes
Of all, love, those who love, like me,
To hear the nightwind as it sighs
Its sweet, yet mournful melody.

And say what image bright and fair,
Now sits on fancy's aerial throne?
What angel sways the sceptre there?
Oh! who but thee my lovely one?

My peerless Lizzy from whose glance
This soul has caught a loving glow,
Unseen,—unspeakable,—a trance
Which weaves its spell where e'er I go!

The breath of morn may fan my brow—
The rills soft music soothe my ear—
The nightwind lifts its voice as now—
Thy loved idea hovers near!

And do those darkfringed eyes still beam,
As lightly as they beamed on me,
When rapt in that delusive dream,
My gaze of worship hung on thee!

And oer that stainless, Parian brow,
Which puts to shame Canova's best,
Say does the ringlet cluster now,
And curl to kiss thy snowy breast?

Oh! there are thoughts beyond revealing,
Which from their depths defy confession,
Oh! there's a tide—a tide of feeling,
Which finds no floodgate in expression!

Thus oft my labouring breast did swell,
As pressed by that unseen emotion,
I've longed—but longed in vain to tell
The glowing tale of my devotion!

Thou'rt absent now sweet girl, but still,
While spreads the vaulted sky above me
Ill cherish that impassioned thrill,
Which bids me never cease to love thee!

votre devoué
[Matieus][2]

RI MS JT/8/2/1/36

1 Elizabeth (Lizzy) Barton, see poem 19, n. 1.
2 *[Matieus]*: the derivation of this apparent nom de plume is not identified.

31 On being caught oversleeping when the postman came *1840s*[1]

Morn was spreading calm and clear
O'er the eastern hemisphere,
Golden curtains hung on high
Hid the blushing orient sky,
Wandering where the streamlet flowed,
Stealing perfume from the rose,
Thence through groves where linnets sing,
Gentle zephyr spread her wing.
Lightly o'er the western hills
Rolled the mist which Night distils,
Rising from his lowly bed
Labour shook his stalwart head,
Brawny bosoms, brown and bare
Drank the gentle morning air,
To the plough the team was strung
In the Vale the Cowboy sung,
Clad in summer vesture gay
Nature smiling blessed the day!

Who is he that slumbers now
Sunshine dancing on his brow
Like a messenger of love
Sent to cheer him from above?
Who that shuts his leaden eyes
To the glory of the skies
On his senseless pillow prone
Dull unprofitable drone
Still inhaling o'er and o'er
Gas which he disgorged before?

Tyndall thou!—the very man
Come, deny it if you can
'Guilty,' 'guilty,' written is
On thy puckered parchment phiz
Oer thy chalk of turnip hue
Blushes murmurs '<u>it is true</u>'!

True by Heaven!—my darling Bob[2]
There I lay a senseless log
Dreaming. Snoozing. Stretching long
Heedless of the skylarks song
When the Postman's heavy tread
Washed the vapours from my head
Ho! what news I cry aloud
Dashing off my blanket shroud
Letters, letters, one two three!
Two from Ginty[3]—one from thee!
How I grasped the welcome prize
Pleasure dancing in my eyes
Welcome as the joyous note
Bursting from the draftsman's throat
Blew the breakfast bugle clear
Falls like music on his ear
Welcome as in days gone by
Was the glance of Allen's eye
Where the thought which spurned control
Shone reflected from his soul
Beaming proudly free and fair
Living independent there!

Oh! I love to dream upon
Nights of toilsome pleasure gone
When mid silence hushed and dread
Slumber shunned my vacant bed
And my cranium over wrought
Panted with its load of thought
When I bent my dewy brow
Oer the page forgotten now
Or with sunken eye afar
Watched the blinking midnight star.

Transient Fancy plumes her wings
From the stupid present springs
Wild regions wandered o'er
By thy friend in days of yore
Memory throws the curtain back
Clears the mortals misty track
Lets the child of Fancy roam

Over times for ever flown
Opens to the backward gaze
All the light of other days
Tinted with a thousand dyes
Caught from richer, happier skies!

To be continued?

RI MS JT/8/2/1/37

1 Perhaps written after he had left Preston (November 1843 for the first time and September 1844 for the second time).
2 *Bob*: possibly Robert (Bob) Allen, who lived in Preston and who had worked for the Irish Ordnance Survey.
3 *Ginty*: William Ginty, see poem 10, n. 1.

32 Tyndall's Ossian *1840s?*[1]

Why sinks into apathy Chadwick's[2]
soul?—Why upon his brow gathers
darkness?—Mourns he for the
past? or flits the ghost of other
days before his mental ken?—
over the memory of friends de-
parted sheds he tears?—my
soul would comfort him!—
with sympathy she swells—oh!
that I were near him—the jocund
laugh should chase the lingering
shadows from his bosom—from
the brow of Tyndall should
flash a ray bright and benig-
nant—glorious as the morning
sunbeam and soothing as the eve-
ning glory which settles on
Compass Hill!!![3]
oh! that I were near him—but
even here my speech would
comfort him—thou friend of
Tyndall, listen!—from his pen
drops balm—like the music
of the honey-bee is his voice,
shedding sweet langour over
the heart—hear Tyndall for
he is mighty to soothe!—
          Dost thou sigh over the
tarnished lustre of thy once
bright drawing pen?—hovers
the shade of the parallel
rulers around thy sleepless
pillow?—or do the mysteries
of the beam compass still burst
upon thy view?—sheds the
sun of other days a glory
round the point of thy once
burnished prickler?—useless
now it lies—coated with rust

is its silvery surface—no more
shall it puncture the snowy
surface of a six inch plan—
gone is the glory of the pricker!
—child of the pensive brow, mourn
not for these—the soul of Tyndall
is sick within him, but from
his sickness shalt thou catch
comfort—darkly lours the cloud
of discontent—around his heart
it lours—turbid is the tide
which swells there—has Chadwick
stood on Phreghane?[4]—has
he seen the mountain billow
rise in the distance?—nearer
and nearer come till with
deadly energy it was anatomised
on the dark Bulman[5]
hast thou not seen the consequent
convulsion?—behold its arch-
etype in the bosom of Tyndall
—the birthplace of the sombre
thought—why swells
thus the breast of Tyndall?—
listen!—over the hosts of the
survey waves the black banner
of tyranny—its shadow is flung
where should else shine the
sun of independence—in the
fell gripe of the oppressor the
sons of the prickler and the pen
do writhe—his eyes round the
cycle of the survey Tyndall casts—thro' its darken
atmosphere beams no star—dark is the horizon
of the survey—
woulds't thou crush its gloom?—No! where
the smile of loved and lovely ones ever greet
thee shall I now dwell—far, far away from
the influence of the sapper's mandate and
the bloody hue of his goatee

RI MS JT/8/2/1/38–9

1 Probably written soon after Tyndall had been sacked from the English Ordnance Survey, in November 1843.

2 *Chadwick's*: see poem 11.

3 *Compass Hill!!!*: a stretch of land in Kinsale overlooking the River Bandon, on the west side.

4 *Phregane*: the headland on the east side of the River Bandon outside Kinsale.

5 *Bulman*: the Bulman pub in Kinsale, situated a few metres from the Atlantic Ocean.

33 [No more dear Bill][1] *1840s*

No more dear Bill the deep blue sea
Its billows lifts twixt you and me
For now on Erin's[2] surfbeat shore
The voice of Tyndall's heard no more
Ive left my fatherland my home
And bounded oer the snowy foam
Ierne's[3] coast has seen my hand
Wave an adieu—a stranger land
Now bears my footprints shall I tell
The thoughts which in my bosom swell
Despair his deepest shadow flings
And sorrow spreads her dewy wings
Where erst dwelt happiness alone
yes, now the heavenly guest has flown
Oh! memory's star with brilliant rays
Sheds lustre over by-gone days
Its golden radiance brightly gleams
Like sunset over burnished streams
But can I hold the burning sigh
Or check the tear which dims mine eye
When fancy paints in colours bright
Those starry eyes transcendent light
So deep—so dark—so eloquent
So mild—so pure—so innocent
Oh! Ginty can I think on this
Nor deeply mourn my withered bliss
Can I forget our last farewell
Can I forget the downy spell
Which softly oer my senses stole
And wound its fibres round my soul
Oh no let others faithless prove
Ill never—never cease to love[4,5]

When last your fancy plumed her pinion
And soared beyond the world's dominion
Sweeping the welkin in her flight
Towards Parnassus cloudy height
There perched upon her roost chimerical
And gazing on the world so spherical

She built a castle wondrous fair
But lo! she built it in the air
This phantom of your [corporation]
This beam of your imagination
This effervescence of your brain
You sent across the darkling main
The breeze from Lancashire and York
Wafted the creature into Cork
I cried with potent exclamation
La! what a monstrous [musereation]
Then as the [brugh] convulsed my throttle
I thought you had embraced the bottle
Which caused the creature to exhale
Mixed with the fumes of English ale
In Tyndalls humble estimation
Your bonds opposed your molestation
By all the scratches of his pen
Bill Ginty is himself again

The instrument of which I write
Placed me in pitiable plight
you called me desolate and drear
you wrapped poor Tyndall in despair
I'll end this portion far too long
By swearing "Ginty you were wrong!"

A trifle now on plumes and prancers
When you and I were embryo dancers
You asped your whispers in the ear
Of Sally[6]—witching little dear
You may call this an antique story
Tis true and truth is Tyndalls glory
the darling heard with many a blush
each overflowing tender gush
And deemed harmonious every note
That blubbered from your rusty throat
Her albums lovely page contained
Effusions by your genius framed
you set before her ravished sight
"We've met when heavenly morn was bright"
And fearing lest the merit due

To your performance should accrue
To other bards you then exclaim
(Insatiable thirst for fame!
Oh! tell it not in Askelon!)
Miss Sally this ere bit's my own
But I will quickly close this scene
nor rake the memories of the green
Where oft "When twilight shadow fell"
you watched with her the ocean's swell
or heard the sweeping surges roar
In madness on the nameless shore[7]

My song which for a [space] did fail
Now wafts my reader to Kinsale
When there arrived you stoutly swore
To us a bombproof heart you bore
"Now boys if me you ever find
"Again by beauty rendered blind
"or hung obeisant on the will
"of woman—cod me then your fill
"Let all your vengeance on me fall
"Ill patiently endure it all"
That human vows are mutable
Is fact quite undisputable
Your high resolve proved passing vain
Frail as a bubble after rain
oh foolish addleheaded boy
Thou good for nothing womans toy
enthusiast you little dreamed
that Ellens[8] eyes in glory gleamed
From when on you her glances fell
Your bows all withered 'neath the spell
And like a donkey to a rod
You bowed submissive to her nod
I own that every warming grace
found shelter in her lovely face
That with the lustre of her eye
The state of even could not vie
I own that her unsullied brow
Was pure as Cheviots purest snow
But what of this—should beauty bind

In fetters an immortal mind
Shall woman—creature of an hour
Unnerve my soul and crush its bower
Bid every generous thought expire
And lead me to a kitchen fire[9,10]

RI MS JT/8/2/1/40–1

1 William Ginty, see poem 10, n. 1.
2 *Erin's*: romantic name for Ireland.
3 *Ierne's*: ancient name for Ireland.
4 Written across the left-hand margin:

> and dares which <1 word erased> [kiss] the sod
> Yet such there is—I marked him well
> His name and nation I could tell
> Ive seen him wrapped in Cupid's trance
> Ive seen him shiver in the glance
>
> Adown his woebestricken cheek
> As oer his fate his bosom yearned
> The mucous in his nostril churned
> And ever and anon would slip
> In yellow ropes adown his lip

5 Written across the right-hand margin:

> Good lack a day and [must I tell]
> Twas Ginty when he sobbed farewell
> and many [again] of purest lay serene

6 *Sally*: unidentified.
7 After this, and before the next section, Tyndall wrote: 'This is no fanciful sketch Ginty—I have not b[illeg]k my imagination to exuberances and left the sombre curtains which shroud futurity—there is nothing ideal in what I have said—could every tooth in Sallys pretty mouth find a tongue a ban for you would foam upon her lips. You proved yourself a sublime rascal in your treatment towards her—pardon me—I must speak the truth—here's at you again—.'
8 *Ellens*: see poem 18, n. 5.
9 Written across the left-hand margin:

> Cou du Conduct

10 Written across the right-hand margin:

> Perish the thought—eternal shame
> Should shroud the [kerry farmers] name
> Who thus would crouch beneath the hand
> of woman and embrace her band
> which chains him to the trodden clod
> *line missing*
> of me,—the truth I can't forego
> tho make play kiss St [Simon's] toe
> La! I have seen the great big tear
> Just like Tom Barrys at a prayer
> In sad sad silence slowly creeps

34 [The past][1] before 13 January 1844[2]

"The past, – the lovely past! – my soul has fed
Upon thine idea, till it has been,
Like light upon the dewy petal shed,
Blent with her very essence, – now I seem
Thy habitant once more, fair Preston, where
The star of Friendship glowed, whose heavenly ray
Oft cheered my heart when shaded o'er by care
And tinged its midnight with the hues of day;
Fair, fleeting dream, too bright, too beautiful to stay!

Preston Chronicle, 13 January 1844
Typewritten transcript only

1 This is one of a series of stanzas sent to *The Preston Chronicle* (the others are lost), under the pseudonym Wat Ripton. The editor wrote: 'WAT RIPTON. – the stanzas sent us by this correspondent, who describes himself as a "distant one," discover considerable poetic feeling, and no small skill in the art of weaving verse. But they have one capital fault, – they are too high flown: sense being, in many instances, sacrificed to sound. One stanza, however, we give – and a very pretty one it is – on account of a local allusion:-.'
2 Tyndall was in Leighlinbridge after being sacked from the English Ordnance Survey.

35 Yet, if to calm ungifted sight[1] *1840s ('after 1843')*

Yet, if to calm ungifted sight
This wizard cell is dread,
What may it be when spells of night
Are through the chamber spread?
When all with gaunt device is rife,
And springs at once to magic life
The heroes of the dead!
To act upon this wondrous spot,
Seems history knew not, or forgot.

=

They come! fresh and living train,
Not vision like, nor pale;
The prince is in his pride again,
The warrior in his mail:
Stern puritan and priest are here,
Gallant and gay, and maid as fair,
As if oblivion's wail
Had never wrapped them in its shade
Nor death had taught their cheeks to fade

=

Yes! in that train is many an one
Whom time shall ne'er destroy;
The brave and gentle "Marmion",[2]
And "Scotland's bold Rob Roy!"[3]
The Lady of Loch Katrine's lake[4]
Where Allan Bane[5] yet seems to wake
His harp to notes of joy;
To think his nature north can claim
One minute of immortal fame!

=

There too a living history
Of Britain seems to pass;
As "Ivanhoe and "Waverley"[6]
Lead on the moving mass:
Whilst he, the great, the mastermind;
Like Banquo's spirit[7] walks behind,
And bears a peopled glass,
Where many a future scene is shown,
And proudly claims them for his own

=

Aye and thine offspring shall be Kings,
Where meaner works shall die,
They only bound of glorious things
:'tis 'immortality!'
Oh, 'tis a proud and goodly page,
Which truth and fiction both engage

To guard and glorify:
Not veiled like hoarded gold or gem
But worn like radiant diadem

=

Now lose the vision lest its rays
"Blast with excess of light!"
As those who in the noontide blaze
Have fixed their dazzled light,
But though the charmed spot ye leave,
The raptured scene will to it cleave,
Until 'tis vanished quite;
And all the earth holds wise or rare
Memory will deem lies treasured there

RI MS JT/8/2/1/44

1 Written at the top of this, in pencil in Tyndall's hand: 'O all these poems are rubbish'.
2 *"Marmion"*: *Marmion; A Tale of Flodden Field*, a poem by Walter Scott (1808).
3 *"Scotland's bold Rob Roy!"*: Rob Roy MacGregor, Scottish outlaw made famous in Walter Scott's novel *Rob Roy* (1816).
4 *Lady of Loch Katrine's lake*: Walter Scott wrote the poem *Lady of the Lake* (1810) after visiting Loch Katrine in the Trossachs, Scotland.
5 *Allan Bane*: Allan-Bane, a minstrel, features in the *Lady of the Lake*.
6 *"Ivanhoe and "Waverley"*: Scottish characters featuring in novels by Walter Scott, published in 1820 and 1814 respectively.
7 *Banquo's spirit*: from Shakespeare's *Macbeth*.

36 Why did I e'er behold thee: A Valentine 13 February 1844[1]

Why did I e'er behold thee
Too lovely as thou art
Why did I e'er allow thee
To steal away my heart
Time was I knew thee not love
A peaceful time for me
Before my eyes met thine love
For then my heart soars free
I think I could forget thee
And give my heart a rest
Which palpitates for thee love
Within this ardent breast
But ah, I try in vain love
From all thy charms to fly
Thou art my life and soul love
And without thee I shall die

RI MS JT/8/2/1/45–6

1 Tyndall was in Leighlinbridge, after having been sacked from the English Ordnance Survey.

37 [Various couplets] *after 1843*

Like a saint ere he enters
Yon realms of delight
While the flames of heaven
Gush full in his sight

He is gone and the valley
Is shadow alone
The purple has vanished
The radiance is gone
Yet the skirts of his mantle
Fall soft on the hill
And the brown crag is smiling
Good bye to him still—

He is gone, and the mountain
Rejoices no more
A pall is flung over
His summit so hoar
And his dark rugged height
From his base to his brow
With its granite tiara
Lies desolate now

He is gone but behold
How the veils of the sky
With their soft silver fringes
Roll silently by
Mid the conclaves of Heaven
A hymn of delight
Is swelling to welcome
The Queen of the night

RI MS JT/8/2/1/48

38 [I tread the land] 29 June 1844[1]

I tread the land that bore me
The green boughs tremble o'er me
When the friends I've tried are by my side
All dangers fly before me!—

A milky parody on Scott[2]—let us try again:—

Ye Squires of Carlow hear me
No cause have ye to fear me
A heart of steel, I'll face the de'il
With George's Nose[3] to cheer me!!!—

RI MS JT/2/1/13; RI MS JT/2/13a/44

1 Written in Leighlinbridge when Tyndall was bidding for the Carlow survey.
2 *A milky parody on Scott*: not identified.
3 *With George's Nose*: Probably a reference to George Latimer's nose. See poem 11, n. 7.

39 The Sky, apostrophe to Friendship[1] 29 July 1844[2]

The sun has fallen beneath the western hill,
And o'er me spreads in slumber deep and still
the wondrous sky, without a single star
To gem its azure bosom—from afar
Phoebus,[3] though bidden, flings a feeble spray,
Quenching their feebler fires in dubious day,
O, holy sky! How beautiful art thou!
Spreading in ages gone as calm as now:
Heaven's balm 'tis thine to gather and to shed,
Like Hermon's dew,[4] upon thy weary head:
Strife is becalmed, the waves of passion cease,
Shamed into quiet by thy tranquil face:
And ever as I fix my sunken eye
In worship on the, O, eternal sky!
Celestial melody, from pole to pole,
Steals soft, in spirit numbers, o'er my soul!

Our sunless atmosphere too weak to chain
The rays shot upward from the western main,
A shade more sable settles on thy brow,
Through which each timid star pales feebly now,
And, like true friendship, but the brighter glows,
As night around thee deeper shadow throws.

Friendship! thy name is empty with the crowd
As sounding brass—a phantasm with the proud;
By others deemed a miscreation fair,
Distilled by poet's brains from upper air—
An essence brighter than the rainbow's hue,
But just as frail and unsubstantial too—
A pretty word to suit a wordy age,
Or grace perchance a sentimental page!

Let those who weave the web of hollow smiles,
And torture nature with a thousand wiles—
Let pride within her chariot cushioned high,
Serenely smiling at the passer-by,
In pity or contempt as veers the gale
Which sets her courtly phantasies asail—

Let the plumed exquisite with clouded cane
And graceful forehead, certified, "Inane"!
Delightful extract of a tailor's shop,
Of sense as guiltless as a scullion's mop
Let soulless, senseless, bipeds such as these
Question thy being, friendship, as they please,
Or deem thee of their own frail, filmy kin,
Prismatic dyes without, but wind within!
Such was the creed of ancient fools who trod
The paths of folly—"Tush! there is no God!"
The Great Unnameable, enthroned high,
Impalpable, unscann'd by carnal eye—
He, the Invisible, whose silent law
Had chastened rebel chaos into awe,
And quarried from its bosom stern and drear
Yon glorious host, and set them shining there—
By owl-eyed folly, blind to reason's beam,
Was held deniable, because unseen!

But say, oh friendship! though thy lovely face
Is veiled where mockeries usurp thy place—
Though bright non-entity thou dost forego,
Shall I prove infidel to thee?—Ah, no!
Though sun-tinged icebergs never felt thy thrill,
My heart of hearts shall hold thee sacred still!
Cold, isolated, must the mortal be,
Whose spirit finds no comeliness in thee.

Sooner than change my lowly lot with him,
Though greaves of gold encircle every limb;
Let me, O Heaven! unheeded let me crawl
My noiseless cycle o'er this earthly ball—
Let cloud or sunshine—weal or woe attend,
This sweetens all—"I still possess a friend!"

Carlow Sentinel 3 August 1844, [4] [5]; RI MS JT/1/HTYP/715
Typewritten transcript only

1 Tyndall sent a short version of this poem, with some word and punctuation changes, to his great friend Thomas Hirst in 1888. He wrote: 'This came in great part back to my memory as I wrote

it. The beginning is cut off. It was headed "The Sky, apostrophe to Friendship". It was written by John 45 years ago, and is now copied for Tom, having been suggested by his last letter' (John Tyndall to Thomas Hirst, 11 April 1888, RI MS JT/1/HTYP/715). This is the original published version.

2 Tyndall was in Leighlinbridge, looking for work.

3 *Phoebus*: Apollo, in Greek and Roman mythology.

4 *Hermon's dew*: a reference to friendship: 'Behold, how good and how pleasant it is for brothers to dwell together in unity! It is like the precious oil upon the head, coming down upon the beard, even Aaron's beard, coming down upon the edge of his robes. It is like the dew of Hermon coming down upon the mountains of Zion;', Psalm 133:1–3.

5 *W.S.*: Walter Snooks, one of Tyndall's pseudonyms, used with *The Carlow Sentinel*.

40 [And must I touch the string][1] 3 June 1845[2]

“And must I touch the string
And woo the muses from their courts above
Traverse the past and wing
From memory a claim upon thy love?” &c.

RI MS JT/2/1/111, RI MS JT/2/13a/83

1 Tyndall wrote in his journal: ‘wrote rhyme to Latimer’ (3 June 1845, RI MS JT/2/13a/83). This is probably George Latimer, who was also working in Yorkshire at the time.
2 Tyndall was living in Halifax, Yorkshire, working as a railway surveyor.

41 [Oh my cottage!][1] 5 June 1845[2]

Oh my cottage! how I mourn
O'er thy dark prospective lot!
Tears, that in their courses burn,
Flow for thee, my pretty cot!

Now the roses cluster round thee
But the time is coming when
Noisome vapours shall surround thee
Who will praise thy beauty then?

Say thou harbinger of sadness,
Glancing through thy level,[3] say
Will you drive my soul to madness
Can you find no other way

Even now mid din & clatter
Fancy hears the 'whistle' swell
Wild as o'er the wreck of matter
Nature poured her dying yell.[4]

Vile embankments—horrid tunnels
Guards & stokers, great and small
Hissing engines—puffing funnels
How I hate you one and all!

RI MS JT/2/1/113; RI MS JT/2/13a/84

1 On this day, while surveying the possible track of a new railway line, Tyndall encountered a woman worried about her cottage. He reassured her that they could go round it (Tyndall Journal, 5 June 1845, RI MS JT/2/13a/83).

2 Tyndall was living in Halifax, Yorkshire, working as a railway surveyor.

3 *Glancing through thy level*: looking through the theodolite.

4 *Nature poured her dying yell*: on 17 July 1846, Tyndall found a copy of Wordsworth's celebrated sonnet against railways enveloping a bundle of cigars, and quoted it in his journal:

"Is there no nook of English ground secure
From rash assaults, schemes of retirement sown
In youth, and mid the busy world kept pure
As when their earliest flowers of hope were blown
Must perish: how can they this blight endure?
And must he too his old delights disown?
Who scorns a false utilitarian line
Mid his paternal fields at random thrown?
Baffle the threat, bright scene from Orrest Head
Given to the pausing travellers rapturous glance
Plead for thy peace thou beautiful romance
Of nature; and if human hearts be dead
Speak passing winds, ye torrents, with your strong
And constant voice protest against the wrong!"
(17 July 1846, RI MS JT/2/13a/133–4)

42 [From the high hill] 2 August 1845[1]

From the high hill—where queenly Catherine
First drew her infant breath, where still are seen
The traces of bygone magnificence
And strength colossal, whose high use is now
Debased and misapplied, in the arch'd halls
Where once the Chieftain's voice resounded and
The light of ladies' eyes shed ecstacy,
The cattle congregate and deem each dim
Polluted chamber shelter from the sun.
From here I gaz'd—westward as if the orb
Drew my eyes thither. Frail is the human tongue
At best: but oh! so frail in me
I dare not whisper of the scene which lay
Before me. But there is a spirit language,
A converse high, which man may hold
With courteous Nature in her haught abodes.
Day had clasped nature in his last embrace,
And, blushing from his first kiss, the empurpled fells
Receded—mass above mass sublime—
Till the most distant blended with the haze
Which like a golden dream encircled all.

RI MS JT/2/13a/96
Typewritten transcript only

1 Written after Tyndall's visit to Kendal and the ruins of the castle in which Catherine Parr was then said to have been born. From Kendal, he walked to Ambleside, and on to see Wordsworth's cottage in the pouring rain. He went to Kendal at the end of July (RI MS JT/2/13a/93) and wrote this in his journal in either Manchester or Halifax or on the train between them on 2 August.

43 [Johnny my dear][1] 9 November 1845[2]

Johnny my dear
I am no engineer
From which you will see
That the letters 'C.E.'[3]
Apply not to me.

Hope whispers a day
Will come when you may
To the letters J.T.
Attach the 'C.E.'!

RI MS JT/1/11/3870–1; John Tyndall to Jack Tidmarsh, 9 November 1845 (letter 325 in TC2). Typewritten transcript only

1 Written to John (Jack) Tidmarsh.
2 Tyndall was based in Halifax, Yorkshire, surveying for a railway line.
3 *C.E.*: Civil Engineer. This poem indicates that Tyndall had in mind becoming an engineer at this stage.

44 Beacon Hill[1] *1840s*[2]

Beacon Hill

Hail to thy hoary summit, ancient friend!
    Whose brown rocks pillar heaven—holding high
Communion with the stars, which nightly bend
    To whisper tales of centuries gone by.

Framed by the haze, and shrouded by the gloom
    Thou cares for neither—rugged titan thou!
Heaven's cloud spread o'er thee like a wargod's plume,
    Finds stern defiance written on thy brow.

Thou brave old hill! From whom the beacon's glare
    Shone like a comet o'er the startled land
Bidding the hardy sons of youth prepare
    To fight for home against each hostile band.

And now as then these homes are worthy all
    The high devotion of true hearted men
And should the clarion of th'invader call
    His belted legions to thy hills again.

To stand in battle for those starry eyes
    To shield their bosoms pure from slight or wrong
You champions of the 'rose of snow' arise
    Die if you must! Ye live in deathless song.

Wat Ripton

RI MS JT 8/2/1/18

1 Beacon Hill overlooks Halifax from the east.
2 Probably written while Tyndall was based in Halifax, between late 1844 and August 1847.

45 [To Fanny][1] 23 August 1846[2]

There is a grace intangible
  An attribute of soul
Which sets details in harmony
  And beautifies the whole
'A mind—a music to the face'
  And tho' the critic sneer
Here dwells thy mystic influence
  Sweet witch of Lancashire

RI MS JT/2/3/82; RI MS JT/2/13a/144

1 Fanny Smith, who Tyndall referred to as 'the Witch', with whom Tyndall had some relationship. Bob Allen told Tyndall she broke off her engagement because of him. See Robert Allen to John Tyndall, 2 July 1847, RI MS JT 2/13a/224–5 (letter 333 in TC2).

2 Tyndall was in Preston, where Fanny Smith lived, after a visit to Ireland and before going back to Halifax.

46 Retrospective poem[1] *c.1845*

Chance led my wandering hands today
Mid dusty papers, grave and gay
Some sparkled with Sam Weller's[2] wit
While here and there were, stewed a bit
Of Cupids rusty prose—again
From George's methodistic pen[3]
Unravelled came a friendly page
A page appeared—a warning page
Of holy love and counsel sage
Next rise to view a pair of poems
From Cuddy's[4] pen, a line from Holmes[5]
Another from Foy,[6] a scratch from Davy[7]
A sheet from Chad[8] as rich as gravy
An invitation to a party
A cherished scrap from Miss McCarthy[9]
A mathematical solution
Of sundry "probs" in evolution
A Valentine where love in roses
A lazy little boy reposes
A rhyme from Ginty[10] when his heart
First felt the little blind boys dart
A curse from ditto loud and long
Another oath and then a song
A shady grove a flowery dell
Moonlight and love from Berkenfell[11]
Another essay most uncivil
Wherein I'm called "an ugly devil"!

RI MS JT/2/5/181–2

1 This poem exists in three very similar versions. It was probably written around 1845, and a version also appears on 10 December 1848 (RI MS JT/2/13b/404), where Tyndall noted in a letter to Ginty that this, written in Halifax, had turned up. He copied it into his journal. The version here is from RI MS JT/2/5/181–2. The others are RI MS JT/8/2/1/51; RI MS JT/2/13b/404.

2 *Sam Weller's*: the pseudonym for John Roberts. See John Tyndall to John Tyndall snr, [3] November 1841, RI MS JT/1/10/3252 (letter 109 in TC1) and a character in Charles Dickens's *The Pickwick Papers* (1836–7). Roberts was discharged from the Irish Ordnance Survey on 9 January 1841. It was on a walk with Roberts that Tyndall christened himself 'Walter Snooks'.
3 *George's methodistic pen*: George Latimer was a Methodist.
4 *Cuddy's*: Martin Cuddy, who had worked with Tyndall on the Irish Survey. Cuddy went to Bandon in May 1841 as part of the Irish Survey's 2nd Division, C District, and stayed there until he was transferred to the English Survey on 8 April 1842 (TC1, 203, n. 3).
5 *Holmes*: George Holmes, who worked with Tyndall on the Irish Survey, before being transferred to the English Survey in May 1842.
6 *Foy*: Thomas Foy, who worked with Tyndall on the Irish Survey.
7 *Davy*: Corporal James Davy, who worked with Tyndall on the Irish Survey.
8 *Chad*: John Chadwick (see poem 11).
9 *Miss McCarthy*: possibly the daughter of Tyndall's landlady at Strand Road, Cork.
10 *Ginty*: William Ginty (see poem 10).
11 *Berkenfell*: see poem 17, n. 3.

47 [A snail crawled forth] September 1846[1]

A snail crawled forth from his darksome cell
    To breathe the scented air
And he looked on the tinges of gold which fell
In softest radiance upon the bell
    Of a flowret bright and fair!

And envy fomenting like yeasty milk
    Thro' his glutinous heart did run
Shall I he cried in darkness sink
While yonder proud and pitiful pink
    Is nurtured by breeze and sun

Onward he went with a felons intent
    This most repulsive snail
Leaving behind his filthy track
While sensitive grass blades started back
    From the touch of his nasty tail!—

He reached at length the flowrets stem
    With malice like rheum in his eyes
It bloomed aloft like a precious gem
Which nature to garnish her diadem
    Had dropped from the golden skies

And then the hate of his jelly race
    Grew darker and sterner still
And he muttered proud pink ere I leave the place
I will climb your stalk and spit in your face
    And sully your beauty—I will—

And his word he kept to his utmost power
    The pink he struggled to gain
But a breeze came in and a sunny shower
Which shook the reptile away from the flower
    To his own vile dust again

Thus Tidmarsh[2] your slime you endeavoured to throw
    With malice prepense upon me
Having shaken you off I will now let you go

As a creature too ugly too wretched and low
        To be crushed by
                        Yours truly
                            J.T.

RI MS JT 8/2/1/53

1 Tyndall was in Halifax, working as a railway surveyor.
2 *Tidmarsh*: John (Jack) Tidmarsh (see poem 9, n. 1 and poem 48). This poem includes three drawings of Tidmarsh's nose.

48 Tidmarsh's nose[1] *c.1846*

Thou ugly sample of the nasal throng
Dirty within and misshapen without
With thee what poet would pollute his song
Thou huge offensive miscreated snout

Thou libel upon all the human race
Unlucky Tidmarsh I to thee appeal
Say why the Furies planted on your face
A type so ugly of an infants heel

I've heard of many beaks & noses queer
Of noses short and pug and large and small
Of noses red and blossomed o'er by beer
But yours in ugliness outshines them all

God wot thy face was ugly quite enough
Then why appeared another foolish feature
Unlucky Tid you have been treated rough
Both nose & face are fulsome peaks of nature—

A fellow sits opposite
Has such a nose
That I cannot really go to bed
Till I compose
A bit of poetry showing its horrible shape
For in truth it belongs to regular ape
It is long—but Oh! Lord it is of such bone
If you saw it you'd stare as if you'd trod on your own
It is short—when compared with its terrible length
In fact it must be a nose of no small beer strength
To stand all the blowings it gets with his wipe
And now I'll give over [a kiss] for the pipe

RI MS JT/8/2/1/54

1 See also poem 47.

49 [The awful 30th][1] 30 November 1846[2]

The day whose grim idea, like a share
        Furrows the brain-box of the engineer
Clutching him from his pillow mid the glare
        Of torturing gas till daylight does appear
Which dawns upon him bending o'er his section
        Like some stray spectre from the resurrection.

RI MS JT/2/3/160, RI MS JT/2/13a/166

1 A reference to 30 November, the deadline for all evidence for Railway Bills to be submitted to Parliament. It caused immense stress to the surveyors, who often had to work round the clock in the days before.
2 Tyndall was in Halifax, Yorkshire, working as a railway surveyor.

50 Acrostic[1] 6 December 1846[2]

B old as the bird of Heaven which soars
O n the rocking cloud when the tempest roars
B raving the lightning's withering tongue
A nd dipping his wing in the whirlwind's womb
L ooking for home where the storm tossed wave
L ashes the walls of some rock spanned cave
E mber of Intellect struck from the sky
N ever, Oh never! to vanish or die!
Wat Ripton

M ild as the gush of infant dawn
A s it steals from the sky to the flowery lawn
G entle and pure as the silver rill
G urgling soft from its moss-clad hill
I s there a bliss which thy Bob could prove
E qual at all to the sum of thy love

RI MS JT/2/3/174–5, RI MS JT/2/13a/167–8

1 For his friends Bob Allen and his wife Maggie.
2 Tyndall was in Halifax, Yorkshire, working as a railway surveyor.

51 The clown and the bees: a fable after the manner of Aesop
28 February 1847[1]

A rompish clown one morning clear
When radiant summer ruled the year
A garden's beauty wished to view
Where buds and blossoms gemmed with dew
Sun-tinted, pearly, pure and fair
Poured their fresh odour to the air
He plucked the tulip from its stalk
And cast it wanton on the walk
Carved "Hodgy Smith"[2] on many a tree
Where blushing fruit hung temptingly
He shook the rosebud from its stem
And soiled the sunflower's diadem
With clog shod feet presumed to tread
Upon the lilly's gentle head.

He reached at length a humming hive
Like fresh-caught cockles "all alive"
Rare sport he cried and cracked a bough
Eh crickey! what a precious row!
In vain the swarming worker's hum
Fell soft upon his thick ear drum
He thrust the twig within the door
And damaged all their little store
At once there rose so wild a yell
The waxy walls of every cell
Gave back an echo full
And rushing forward right pelmel
Upon th'invading foe they fell
Who often wished himself in Hell
    Or Halifax or Hull!

A thousand stings gleamed wildly round
A cloud of wings upon him frowned
The bowels of that hive profound
    Disgorged a countless throng
His arms around are vainly flung
Upon his nose the queen bee hung

Within his ear a cohort sung
Around his eyes a dozen clung
The lilly bells an echo rung
        To curses deep and strong!

The sun is up he sees it not
His eyes are bunged—he damns his lot
Sky, earth and air and grove & grot
Are one illimitable blot
He turns blindly from the spot
        And rushes through my song

To Ginty[3]—The application to come?

RI MS JT/2/3/224; RI MS JT/2/13a/180–1

1 Tyndall was in Halifax, Yorkshire, working as a railway surveyor.
2 *"Hodgy Smith"*: not identified.
3 *Ginty*: William Ginty. See poem 10.

52 [The joys and the wishes][1] 11 March 1847[2]

"The joys and the wishes
The loaves and the fishes
On which you so wantonly revel
Will go—and quite right—
To the people's delight
Most exceedingly quick to the Devil!"
Wat Ripton
Ex. Gov. official

RI MS JT/2/3/239; RI MS JT/2/13a/185

1 Fragment, probably by Tyndall, in a letter to the Editor of *The Sligo Champion* (which appears not to have been published). The political context is given in letter 328 in TC2.

2 Tyndall was in Leighlinbridge visiting his father, who died on 27 March, three days after Tyndall had to return to England.

53 Society 27 July 1847[1]

Though to the common eye my lot may seem
Uncheered and lonely,—though the lovely spell
Which works in woman's eyes points not to me,
Nor woman's tongue to the material ear
Appeals in music—still I'm not alone.
Pale is my cheek, perchance, and somewhat scarred
By inwards workings, whence the crowd might deem
My thoughts unhappy; yet it is not so.
I lack not sweet companionships; my soul
Has the society of those she loves:
Over the graves of buried years she treads,
And, from their amber coffins, ancient eyes
Beam lovingly upon her,—audible to her ears
the deep-toned whispers of the mighty dead
Sound like cathedral bells! Nor need she seek,
Amid the debris of departed times,
For genial company: even now she holds
Intense communion with the peopled world,
And clasps in friendship the immortal hands
Of godlike man. The glowing Cadmean page,
Poured from its great composer's prodigal brain,
Spreads like an ocean, whose unbounded waves
Mirror soft rainbows, and expend their force
In dulcet music on celestial shores!

Dark clouds may gather, hostile thunder roll,
And, buffeted by fortune, I may seem
Outcast from joy. Suspend thy sapient sneer,
O man of many pounds! exulting still,
My spirit treads upon the Andean tops,
Superior to the storm which crushes thee.

Beautiful Nature! boundless source of bliss,
To those whose souls are tuned to thy sweet tongue:
With eyes more true than woman's, pouring light
Over empyreal hills! My queen, my bride!
Whose love is changeless as the eternal source
From whence thy beauty springs,—I am thine own,
Wholly and undivided: and when fate

Strikes this organic structure to the dust,
Like a freed slave my spirit shall arise,
Throw her unmanacled arms around thy neck,
And lose herself within thy smile for aye!

Preston Chronicle, 10 July 1847, [3], signed Wat Ripton
Typewritten transcript only

1 Tyndall was in Halifax, Yorkshire, soon to leave for his teaching job in Queenwood College, Hampshire.

54 [All smatterers are more brisk and pert][1]
2 June 1848[2]

all smatterers are more brisk and pert
Than they which understand an art
As little sparkles shine more bright
Than glowing coals which give them light

RI MS JT/1/T/515; John Tyndall to Thomas Hirst and James Craven, 2 June 1848 (letter 348, TC2)

1 According to Melinda Baldwin and Janet Browne (letter 348, n. 5 and n. 6, TC2) this is derived from *Hudibras*, a poem by Samuel Butler, satirising the Presbyterian Church and the Parliamentary position on the Civil War. These lines, written in the context of the need for modesty and humility when tackling problems, do not appear in the poem. The letter leads in with: 'Tom's remarks as to the necessity of modesty are quite correct but Hudibras says:'
2 Tyndall was at Queenwood College, Hampshire, preparing to leave on a visit to Paris.

55 [Our seasons of joy] 31 July 1848[1]

Our seasons of joy
Are like flowers on the mountain
Far beneath lies the treasure,
The life giving fountain
We may gather our flowers
At ease in the sun
By the sweat of our brow
Must the other be won
Labour then
Fellow men
Up brave hearts, try again
Ours is no struggle for might or domain
Ours no ignoble strife
Aiming at purer life
Front we all hardships, all trial, all pain!

RI MS JT/2/5/89–90; RI MS JT/2/13b/372

1 Tyndall was at Queenwood College, having returned from Paris and Brussels, and gave his first lecture in physics on this day.

56 Alone 29 December 1848[1]

There is a kind of music in the word,
Which, like a storm at night, swells in the soul
Mysterious joy. The massive druid stones,
The crumbling castles of our native land,
Upon whose shoulders Time his strata builds,
Are lonely, all; yet, here though latent, live
Electric memories, and men are roused
To valour by appeals to these old walls.
The tombs of ages! voices from the dead
Find sympathetic echoes in the heart,
And man is more than man when thus he dwells
Amid the wrecks and ruins of the world!
But, higher, still, the rapture which he feels,
When 'mid the wonders of the universe,
His soul unpinioned soars, to be alone
Upon the high, untrodden, mountain top,
Where the winds whistle and the pine-trees moan,
Amid the solemn grandeur of the night,—
It is not joyless thus to be alone.
The joylessness is his whose glossy eye
Depicts eternals faithful as the lens,
Whose iris can refract the slanting ray,
And retina receive the landscape fair,
And nothing more,—who sees no loveliness
Under the tinted surface of the leaf,
Behind the crag, beyond the star no life,
Shining through Nature's features as the gleam
Which lights the eye and beautifies the cheek
When an o'erflowing love is in the heart.

They talk of pleasures which I, too, have proved,
And kindly ask me here and there to join
The banquet and the dance; and I have gone,
And laughed my share and listened to the song,—
Described the mazy waltz, and schooled my lungs
Into the soft cadences, to win the ear
Of lovely woman, thinking this was bliss,
And that the gods no higher could bestow:
Yet was it evanescent as a dream,

Which melts like frost-work in an infant's hand.
I censure not, decry not; but, let me,
Myself, unravel from the tortuous throng,
With free stretched pinion, let my spirit fly
Like the strong mountain-bird to its own hills;—
The world my banquet room, the floating clouds,
Fringed with the amber of the setting sun,
The curtains of my chamber, and the stars,
Nailed to the deep blue ceiling of the sky,
My substitute for gas. Thus—thus, alone,
The ministering angels swoop from heaven
And whisper joy, the shadows disappear,
And life is light—thine eyes, sweet girl, which once
Sent through the succulent fibres of my heart
Electric bliss, and served, perchance, to guide
My footsteps for a time, wax pale and dim
Amid the brightness of my present day!
Listen! The hills are singing, vocal all;
The cloud, the crag, the torrent, and the tree,
The wild wind piping to the stars its song,
The spirit voices of the universe,—
All call me friend, and bid me welcome here.

One thing, alone, worth aught can man bestow—
His gold? I need it not—my own right hand
Shall carve my daily bread, therewith content.
But, that last relic of primeval bliss,
Which still to man amid his ruin clings—
His LOVE—to me is precious as my breath.
And here I can't complain, I bless the gods
For loving hearts; and when I call to mind
The banks of Ribble,[2] from the terraced slope
Of Avenham,[3] to Red Scar's lovely sweep,[4]
I people them with friends and faces dear.
Already thought forestalls the work of time
And ante-dates the seam upon my brow,
But touches not my heart,—its amaranth
Blooms on, unfading, and gives love for love!

Preston Chronicle, 13 January 1849, p. 3.[5]

1 Tyndall was in Marburg, studying for a PhD.
2 *Ribble*: The River Ribble flows through Preston, Lancashire.
3 *Avenham*: in Preston.
4 *Red Scar's lovely sweep*: near Preston.
5 The version in Tyndall's journal is somewhat different. See also RI MS JT/2/5/191–4; RI MS JT/2/13b/407–9.

57 [There is no cloud in heaven tonight][1] 31 December 1848[2]

There is no cloud in heaven tonight
    The moon is empress there
And the stars are glancing keen and bright
    Through the clear and frosty air

Far far from the roof where my youth was reared,
    And far from my childhood's home,
And far from my father's silent grave,
    I ponder all alone

The stinging tear is in mine eye
    And the grief is in my heart
As each trace of hope is smitten away
    When I think of what thou art.

O, art thou gone, for ever gone,
    Shall I see thy face no more
From the echoing tombs of the old churchyard[3]
    Comes the sad reply "No more".

Low he lies all crumbling there
    Arm and chest and limb
The moonbeams cold, or the sundawn fair
    Shall shine no more on him.

Oh, I was a dweller within thy heart
    Ere it was changed to clay
And my name was on thy bloodless lips
    When thou wert snatched away.

But now the light is quenched and gone
    Which cheered my endeavours here,
And I must plod through life alone
    And smother the useless tear.

Yet there is an essence survives his shroud
    And defies the dart of death,

Which vanishes not as the morning cloud
        Nor flies with the fleeting breath.

He made no will, he had nought to leave
        A struggler poor was he,
But the royal stamp of an honest man
        Was his legacy to me.

Erect among men my father stood
        His son shall do the same
He shall live by God's help as true a life
        And die with as fair a name.

The last pulse beat of the dying year
        Rings out from yon mountain head.
Hark, the shouts of man and the roar of guns
        Proclaim that the year is dead!

RI MS JT/2/5/201–3; RI MS JT/2/13b/412

1 Written thinking about his father, who had died the previous year.
2 Tyndall was in Marburg, studying for a PhD.
3 *From the echoing tombs of the old churchyard*: Tyndall's father was buried in the churchyard of St Laserian's Cathedral, Old Leighlin, Carlow.

58 [I cannot write of love as poets do][1] 22 April 1849[2]

I cannot write of love as poets do
Not twist the little iron I possess
To wires of agony. I cannot pour
My molten spirit on the artistic sand
Whose wrinkles are expression, I have built
Within my breast a plain domestic hearth
Where the sweet memory of an absent friend
Kind word, fair face, or honorable act
May dwell unfrozen. Still I sometimes feel
A hint of powers I would not verify
A kind of earthquake rumble in my soul
Portending fire below, but reason still
With granite arms has clasped the turbulent waves
And kept their forces down, or haply is't
The lack of circumstance which yet may come
Loose hounds of passion, wasteful as the storm,
Which throttles ocean like a tortured bull
And shakes my circumspection into rags.
[Correct this you dog!]

RI MS JT/2/5/239; RI MS JT/2/13b/425

1 Tyndall wrote this poem in his journal, following a comment about Emerson: 'To the accountant and man fond of comforts the writings of Emerson are false because unintelligible, he asks proofs but can receive none. the narrator is not asked to prove his adventures by the rules of logic, he describes what he has seen and heard; would the querist know the truth he must visit the region himself.'

2 Tyndall was in Marburg, studying for a PhD.

59 [Brave hills of Thuring] 28 May 1849[1]

And here he dwelt,[2] whose mighty voice, like thunder,
Shook the proud battlements of Rome asunder;
Here paused, perchance like me, when day was failing,
Watching the bright-edged clouds through heaven sailing,
Tracking the swallow in its course so cheery,
Cleaving the stilly air with wing unweary,
Fixing his glance upon the western glory,
Beaming aslant upon these mountains hoary.
Brave hills of Thuring! or with forests planted,
Bearing aloft your oaken brows undaunted,
Or stark and grim upholding summits dreary,
Where the wild eagle loves to build his eyrie,—
Stout orators! who stir the gazer's spirit
With the wild energies your crags inherit,
Who nerved those stalwart thoughts which fell like granite
Upon the caked traditions of our planet,
Crushing, despite her terrors, stakes and lashes,
Rome's ancient formulas to dust and ashes!
And here he sat, and here he paused and pondered,
Gazed from those heights, and through those valleys wandered,
And once, when leaning o'er this ancient table,
As midnight clothed the world in robes of sable,
His candle waned—a shudder curdled o'er him,
When lo! the Prince of Darkness stood before him.
A moment's fear,—'tis gone—and Heaven-reliant
He lowered upon the fiend a brow defiant:—
"Or com'st thou, by permission, here to try me,
Or deputy from hell to terrify me;
The effort's vain—I fear thee not—I'll face thee,
And as an earnest, Oh, thou son of Evil!
Take that."—He shied his inkstand at the devil!

'A Whitsuntide Ramble', *Preston Chronicle*, 16 June 1849, [3][3]

1 Tyndall wrote this poem in Luther's Room at the Wartburg near Eisenach. He copied it out again on 19 June 1871 in Folkstone and on 21 June 1871, the day he left Folkestone after a week's

break to visit Mary Egerton. He then posted a third copy of the poem, of which a fragment remains, to James Clerk Maxwell (see Jackson 2018, 322). The envelope is dated 27 June 1871 from Cambridge and was presumably forwarded on to Maxwell in Scotland. Tyndall was observing the lighthouse at Howth Bailey, in Ireland, that day but had been in London a couple of days previously.

2 *And here he dwelt*: the poem is a homage to Luther, exiled to the Wartburg near Eisenach, who translated the New Testament from Greek into German. To banish his vision of Satan he famously threw an ink-well at it. Tyndall wrote a lengthy description of his visit in his journal (RI MS JT/2/13b/433–5).

3 There are several other versions: RI MS JT/2/5/261–2 (28 May 1849); RI MS JT/2/13b/434–5 (28 May 1849, typescript copy); RI MS JT/8/2/1/55–71 (two copies, made on 17 and 19 June 1871). In addition there is the fragment sent to James Clerk Maxwell on 27 June 1871 (CU Add 7655/VI/3 (vii)), which reads as follows:

top of page cut off, with half of one missing line illegible, then:

Or o'er the foliage lifting summits dreary
Which the bold eagle chooses for his eyrie.
Mute presences! who quell the gazer's spirit
A measure of the strength your crags inherit
In front of you he stood when day was failing
Watching the listed clouds through azure[3o] sailing
Tracking the swallow in its course so cheery
Clearing the stilly air with wing unweary.
With eye and heart sublime as fell the glory
From the red west upon their ridges hoary.

Fit [nurses] of the thoughts which fill like [p. ...]
Upon the caked had[illeg] of our planet.

----

60 To McArthur[1] 17 September 1849[2]

Were not our universe so rich I'd mourn
Thy sudden disappearance from among
Our ranks on earth—But nature leans on none,
And choice as was thy texture can refill
Thy vacant post—yet does thy early blight
Thy sad extinction reach me like the sound
The low sad wailing of the autumn wind
Laden with grief—clear head and noble heart,
The free drawn outline of an able man,
I saw in thee—Oh little understood
Conceived of through thy failings by the herd
Whose grosser organs cannot penetrate
The inward essence of a man like thee
Pronounced unholy, wretched, unredeemed,
Nay haply doomed—but what of that reekst thou
Brother of the Eternities no more
To mingle with the clangour of the day
Sleep sweetly till we come and O ye stars,
In decent silence sentinel his grave!—

RI MS JT/2/5/295; RI MS JT/2/13b/447

1 McArthur was a friend of Tyndall and his colleagues in Yorkshire. He was apparently a heavy drinker of gin, and died after taking poison. See John Tyndall to Thomas Hirst, [2 July 1849], RI MS JT/1/T/520 (letter 0379 in TC2).

2 Tyndall was in Marburg, about to set off on a long walking trip that would take him into Switzerland for the first time.

61 My story of "the Screen"[1] c.1891 but originally written much earlier[2]

Large has my love for Nature been,
        I loved her from a child
I loved her in her summer sheen
        And when the winter wild
Wrapped storms around her awful brow,
        And ocean formed a throne
To bear her, Queen and conqueror,
        My love was her's alone

RI MS JT/3/38

1 The Screen was Tyndall's huge edifice erected near his house in Hindhead, to shield him from the view of his neighbour's stables. See Jackson 2018, 442, 446, 448.

2 Tyndall notes: 'Thus I wrote in my Lehrjahren. The lines are worthless but they mark a tendency.' The writing of 'Lehrjahren' in German suggests that this was perhaps written in Marburg.

62 [Common the hum of the bee] c.1850[1]

[2]"Common
the hum of the bee
the torrid zone between two
temperate ones.

Tinted leaves of beech

Ball
We all have our periods of doubt and darkness, of laziness
perhaps, but the habit is the thing."[3]

RI MS JT/2/6/319; RI MS JT/2/13b/659

1 Possibly around 1850 but copied into his journal on 11 February 1854, when Tyndall was in London.
2 Before this, in his journal, Tyndall wrote: 'Found my pocket book which contains my notes of some of Faraday's experiments. On opening it I find written in pencil on the first page I look at the following cabalistic words.'
3 After this, in his journal, Tyndall writes 'I do not know where or in what circumstances these words were written.'

63 On the death of Dean Bernard[1] 29 March 1850[2]

The sun is gone, and night her shadowy robe
Throws round the east, upon whose sable brow
Arcturus sparkles like a fiery gem.
Yonder, Orion clasps his starry belt
About his mighty loins and stalks thro' Heaven.
Great Sirius flames, and right above my head,
Capella twinkles—eastward whirls the Bear,
Around yon solitary globe of light,
Firm axled in the north—its silent home,
Myriads of ages ere the creator's thought
Found an incorporate utterance in Man.
Aye, all is stable there—they come and go,
Beholding races perish, states decay,
Creeds vanish, temples crumble in the dust,
Chartered by God to walk the Universe
Unchanged by centuries; while feeble man,
Mutative as the breeze, sees every hour
Laden with new-born grief. A while ago
I was a son—that sound is senseless now,
For he has disappeared, and moonlight teems
Its silver on his grave. And now again
A knell sweeps o'er the surface of the Rhine,
Whose emerald waters shiver in the sound,
As if reluctant to revive the throb,
So lately stilled.

Gone to return no more
Guide of my youth, my counsellor, my friend!
A drear bewilderment has settled in my brain,
And startled fancy shudders to convey
The total import of those fearful words—
"He's dead!" What means it? To be seen no more,
And heard no more;—the gentle cadence hushed,
The mild eye quenched eternally—extinct!
Infinite distance in a moment spread
Twixt him and me. A stupor steeps my sense,
My soul reels baffled from the vain attempt
To solve all this—Almighty, what is man?
The puppet of thy sufferance sublime,

A water drop, which, loosened by thy breath,
Glitters a moment o'er the eternal wave,
Then seeks the boundless deep from whence it came.
God's goodness, in a mild incarnate form,
Revealed itself in thee—sent down to cheer
The orphan's heart, and wipe the widow's eye
But thou are gone; and widows' tears may flow
And orphans' sighs invite thee back in vain.
Where gone? Hence incubus! *that* is not he
Which moulders in yon dark and narrow hole!
Oh! *thou* wert the inscrutable handiwork of God,
Within it placed, unseen by sensuous eye,
And unexplainable by human thought.
Thy scaffolding it was, but not thyself
A mystic organ officered by *thee*
Unsharing its derangements thou hast laid
The weary coil aside, and sought again
Thy father's house—that many-mansioned dome
Eternal in the Heavens. There to dwell
Nor stoop from thy empyreal heritage
To share earth's clangor.—Spirit, Friend—Farewell!

'On the death of Dean Bernard', *Carlow Sentinel*, 13 April 1850, [4][3]

1 Richard Boyle Bernard, or Barnard (1787–1850), was the second son of Francis, Earl of Bandon. After studying at Cambridge and being called to the Bar, he returned to the family seat and served as MP for Bandon Bridge, County Cork, from 1812 to 1815. He subsequently vacated his Parliamentary seat and was ordained as a priest. In 1820 he became rector of Glankeen, County Cashel, and two years later he was appointed Dean of Leighlin and was based at the Cathedral Church of St Laserian in Old Leighlin. Tyndall and his father considered Barnard a useful and reliable patron. This is the only one of Tyndall's published poems with the byline of his own name. All the others are given under pseudonyms, except 'From the Alps: a fragment', the original version of 'A morning on Alp Lusgen' (see poem 76), which uses his initials J.T.

2 Tyndall was in Marburg when he heard of Dean Bernard's death.

3 There are also handwritten and typescript versions: RI MS JT/2/5/383–5; RI MS JT/2/13b/483.

64 [Hail to thee, mighty runner!][1] 12 December 1852[2]

Hail to thee, mighty runner! before whom my senses reel
The greyhound's foot is fleet but O! it lags behind thy wheel
The soaring eagle steeps his breast in yon etheral sea
And cleaves the tempest with his wing but yields the race to thee.
Oh who can chain his sweating limbs or curb his stormy speed
When the stoker stirs his courage up our gallant iron steed!

In Lincoln it is true my friends, there lives a rusty wight
I purpose no offence against the town of Mr Wright[3]
But a hundred thousand Sibthorps[4]—my brothers what are they
When they dare to check our charger bold he tramples them like clay
And scatters them my brothers mid the thunder of the train
As the roaring lion shakes the dew at morning from his mane!

Oh! tis glorious lads to see him when the darkness spreads around,
And his fiery eye-balls glisten as he stretches o'er the ground.
Like the sound of many waters he rushes through the vale
And the crags around re-echo to the rattle of the rail.
With his banner-cloud of vapour high over him unfurled
He makes the mountains shiver boys and jostles with the world!

But most of all should Mr Haas[5] admire our courser brave
For it carried him to Jersey in the teeth of wind and wave
And though it made his stomach reel the sickness soon was o'er
When it landed him in safety on that hospitable shore
Where wine is got for nothing and you're paid for drinking beer
Oh! could we shelve our books my boys and make a Jersey here!

And when the thoughts of mountain homes came crowding on his mind
What carried him to Switzerland thrice quicker than the wind?
And back again triumphant o'er the billows of the sea
To steam and wheels Oh! Mr Haas right grateful should you be
I mourn your country Mr Haas with all its heights sublime
Where the hardy ferns cluster and the stalwart mountain pine
For we cannot tunnel through those rocks so obdurate & hard
And a single line of rails (÷) is all that's left unto the bard.

And Christmas too is coming boys when ivy-berries shine
In hospitable welcome o'er the wallnuts and the wine.

Hail to the great magician who will carry us away
From problems, nouns, and chemicals upon that happy day
When school breaks up and every boy is dreaming how
He will kiss his little cousin underneath the mistletoe bough
And hail to him my brothers! when his whistle sounds again
To bear us back to fight the fight of gallant little men
To beat old Euclid under us and conquer every foe
Fresenuis,[6] Arnold,[7] Hutton,[8] Haas, and Mr Colenso![9]

(÷) Between Baden and Zürich

RI MS JT/2/6/169–71; RI MS JT/2/13b/590–1

1 Tyndall called this 'a scrap written for Borlase to conclude his lecture on the steam engine'. Borlase is not identified, but may have been a teacher at Queenwood College.
2 Tyndall was based at Queenwood College at this time.
3 *Mr Wright*: perhaps Tyndall's Queenwood colleague was born in Lincoln.
4 *Sibthorps*: Colonel Charles Sibthorp (1783–1855), born in Lincolnshire, was a Tory politician who believed that railways were a fad and the country would soon return to stagecoaches.
5 *Mr Haas*: John Haas was a teacher at Queenwood with Tyndall. He had previously taught at Fellenberg's Hofwyl School in Switzerland.
6 *Fresenuis*: possibly Carl Remigius Fresenius (1818–97), a German analytical chemist.
7 *Arnold*: not identified.
8 *Hutton*: possibly James Hutton (1726–1797), Scottish geologist.
9 *Mr Colenso!*: possibly John William Colenso (1814–83), mathematician and theologian, though this poem predates his controversial writings.

65 [The heights of Science] 6 December 1853[1]

The heights of Science woo me, and I clamber
With patient strides the mountain's rugged back
At times o'er flinty boulders slowly wending
Beat by the storm while clouds obscure my track.
Weary it is to wander thus so lonely
And mighty must that mystic instinct be
Which prompts my toil, commanding ever onward!
Drowning dismay in stern necessity.
My feet are sore but yonder is the summit
Rough clouds and chasms loom athwart my way
[2]Into the clouds Oh worker!—brave the labour
Rest is beyond—not here—away! away!
"You must proceed!" Oh! who can truly measure
The bone and muscle of a brave self-trust
The might and compass of a man's endeavour
Till scourged to action by a strong "you must!"
A deadly whisper to the coward hearted
A challenge to the brave who loves to try
The metal of his manhood in the conflict
With circumstance, which shapes his destiny.

RI MS JT/2/6/294; RI MS JT/2/13b/643–4

1 Tyndall was in London, but wrote in his journal that this was 'scribbled in the lining of my hat one morning walking along the Lahn', so it was probably originally written in October 1848 to June 1850 or October 1850 to April 1851, as Tyndall was tempted by a career in science.

2 There is a marginal note in pencil (probably by Louisa):
[The might & majesty of man's endeavour
when scourged to actions by the stern "I must"
is a version I have read somewhere else
L.]

66 Dear Tom, the sky is gray 7 March 1854[1]

Dear Tom, the sky is gray
Today:
And like a vapour dense and dull
Something within my scull
Weighs heavily upon my aching brain.—
Would that the mind could rain!
And thus discharge in one full shower the weight
Which cumbers me of late.
Would that thou hadst a horse
To bound o'er grass and gorse
And make a breeze, though none should stir in heaven
I'd start before eleven
Next Sunday with the bridle in my hand,
And gallop o'er the land
The wind should stir the hair
Around my temples fair
And the bright crimson to my pale cheek bring
Till maids should long to kiss so fair a thing.
And then the whisker's span
Sublime appendix! which thou canst but scan
On cheeks like mine,
Denied alas! to Debus's[2] and thine
Or, half ashamed to be espied
Pays Haas[3] a furtive visit at one side!
finis

Elton Hall Archive; RI MS JT/1/HTYP/324 (typed transcript)

1 Tyndall was in London. He copied this into his journal 10 days later, on 17 March. See RI MS JT/2/6/333; RI MS JT/2/13b/667.
2 *Debus's*: Heinrich Debus (1824–1915), a chemist who taught at Queenwood College.
3 *Haas*: John Haas, see poem 65, n. 5.

67 Meditations before breakfast 4 March 1855[1]

Without, the Heaven's grand Engineer
Has bent his dome so wide and high
Within, four panels [(x)] shining clear
Compete in colour with the sky.
Without, the white frost crystals shed
Their lustre in the morning glow
Within, the linen on my bed
Transcends the frost and rivals snow.
Without the larks and linnets dear
Sing sweetly to the morning star;
But Oh! meseems thy silence here
My bonnie room is sweeter far.
Oh! I would give for this small span
Far, far, from London's smoke and din,
Where whispering angels speak to man
Whose words are lost in yonder din.
Yes, I would give,—but ah! not mine
The right—sweet Anna[2] must I speak?
I'd give—great Tom[3] thine ear incline—
I'd give, by jove! five bob a week!

[(x)] in the door.

RI MS JT/2/7/25–6; RI MS JT/2/13b/732

1 Tyndall was on a weekend break in Queenwood College, where he wrote this poem.
2 *Anna*: Anna Hirst, who had married Thomas Hirst on 27 December 1854. She died of tuberculosis on 1 July 1857.
3 *Tom*: Thomas Hirst.

68 [God bless thee Poet!][1] 7 August 1855[2]

God bless thee Poet! while the dewy tear
Shines in my eyes, and with expanded arms
And shuddering joy I drink thy melody
Murmuring 'beautiful!' I bless thy voice,
Thy perfumed voice which searches me all through,
Which kills my apathy and plants new life,
New hope, new strength, new beauty in my heart.
God bless thee! let me hear thee oft—Oh! come,
When the cold brain o'erbalances the soul,
When intellect untinctured by a hue
Of feeling deems all Nature a machine,
And life itself the product of a force
Which acts it knows not why,—Thou mak'st me feel
A force beyond the force which science knows—
A life beyond her life, whose mystic seeds
Are songs, thy songs Oh! fragrant brother mine,
Which cause the heart to blossom where they fall.

J. T.

RI MS JT/2/7/257; RI MS JT/2/13b/799

1 Tyndall wrote in his journal: 'The following may be pleasant to me at some future day and I therefore copy it to save it from being lost. I wrote it in a blank scrap of Tennyson's Maud' (RI MS JT/2/13b/799). It is presumably a homage to Tennyson, who Tyndall did not meet until 1858.

2 Tyndall was in London.

69 The morning bell[1] 27 October 1855[2]

Oh how I love thy silver tones melodious morning bell
When through the long drawn corridors thy mellow pulses swell
With voice each morn thrice sweeter than the famed Orphean fife
Thou makest every coverlet to ripple into life.

I start, great bell, when thou dost call, with all my vigour roused;
I stand with ten boys' energies within my muscles housed,
And bless thee as thy dulcet tones upon my senses fall,
And drop a tear when thy dear tongue is silent in the hall!

They talk of harps and fiddles—of flute and deep bassoon;
They talk of songs which nightingales perform to please the moon;
But ne'er on mortal tympanum a softer music fell,
Than thine—thou joy of all the boys—delicious Morning Bell!

Our Cornwall[3] tickles every string with light elastic hand,
Our Haas[4] in his peculiar way is wonderfully grand,
And Dr Hirst,[5] with lengthy arm and equally long bow,
Brings music from the bowels of his Violincel—lo;

But thou dost topple o'er them all as pine tree o'er a weed;
Thou art a blowing rose, and they mere charlock gone to seed.
Beef to the Ringer! Give him strength to do his duty well,
And charm us with the sweet ding dong—the boys' beloved Bell!

ONE OF THE BOYS

The 'bell' to say the truth, is considered a peculiarly dismal affair by the boys.

The Queenwood Observer (31 October 1855), vol. 3, no. 8, p. 68; RI MS JT/2/7/205–6; RI MS JT/2/13c/798

1 Written for *The Queenwood Observer*, the school magazine. Tyndall wrote in his journal: 'Having promised Beck to write something for the Observer, one night returning from the

Lodge my promise occurred to me. The night was cool and calm and speech came to me' (RI MS JT/2/13c/798).

2 Tyndall was based at Queenwood College for around a month at this time.

3 *Cornwall*: [John] Cornwall, the music master (Hirst Journal, RI JT 2/32c/1166).

4 *Haas*: John Haas, see poem 64, n. 5.

5 *Dr Hirst*: Thomas Hirst, an accomplished cellist and pianist.

70 [Ballad of the Isle of Wight] 30 June and 1 July 1856[1]

At 7. the sound of preparation ceased
For breakfast—we attacked it—Wright[2] and I
And Mrs Wright, and Allman[3] a young celt;
They to their tea, I to my cocoa mild
Which Mrs Leary[4] mixes every morn
With milk thus forming a nutritious mud
For like to water charged with silica
Which lodged within the caverns of the earth
Turneth to flint, so tea within the dome
Of my deep stomach seemeth turned to stone
And lies a heavy nodule on my heart.
A chop this morn kind Mrs Wright prepared
For us; while Allman whose stomachic juice
Can deal with stiffer matter, fed on ham.
At half past 7 our little chariot wheels
Crunched the loose gravel opposite our door,
And we took up our places; Wright and I
To make the strain upon the pony less,
Took the front seat, with Mrs Wright behind.
We only three—for Allman young and lithe
Scattered his convex limbs towards Bournemouth.
"What glorious weather! see you" I exclaimed
"A single cloud, or trace of cloud, to spot
The cobalt of the sky?" "No", not a trace—
But yes—see there is one! cried Mrs Wright
I looked aloft and saw the floating snow
High up in heaven; as if a thoughtful saint
In white apocalyptic linen clad
To whom the earth had been a place of love
And beauty in the pleasant summer time,
Had left angelic concerts to revive
Acquaintance with the lark, and warm his soul
With the dear memory of terrestrial joys.
We passed the gate where the mean mortar sphynx
Turns her cracked buttocks from the morning sun
As if ashamed to let the rosy dawn
Shine on the shabbiness of painted clay.
Forward through Milton Green, where Wright and I
Some days before enjoyed a pint of beer

And the sharp twinkle of a female eye
Of doubtful radiance; so at least thought Wright,
And I, though all unskilled, inferred the same.
Onward! alighting where the slopes hung steep;
And once at such a time I walked beside
A slow old man, on whose blue jacket gleamed
Two silver medals, and I asked him where
He had obtained them: "in the wars" he said
"On the Peninsula five years I fought
And struck my man at bloody Waterloo
Dear Sir the crops were good for many a year
With the rich dung we scattered on that day".
Onward again until the clustering roofs
Of Lymington appeared: the cleanly walls
And painted shutters which today were up
In honour of the Queen,[5] the sober air,
To me were pleasant for a human voice
Is here a sound, not broken, swamped and lost
As in the growl and clash of London wheels.
And as we trotted down the street
Through the laburnum tracery there gleamed
Two faces which seemed fair, and bright with smiles
The hindering foliage passed I looked again
For beauty of my heart confers a boon
Whether it be a landscape or a child
Or sprouting maiden on whose tender face
The soul makes music, blending with her voice.
And so I looked—the false laburnum green
Had thrown a glare subjective in my eyes
Which made the ugly fair; for I saw through
The unimpending air two wenches coarse
Who grinned and nodded at me as I gazed.
I cursed their impudence, and moodily
Looked at the townclock—it was half past nine.
We put our pony in the hostler's hands
And told him to be bountiful with corn
And charge each fibre of the beast with force
To bear us homeward cheerily at eve.
We reached the steamer where with heart of fire,
Though motionless, she lay—a human swarm
Already filled her decks, and me to swell

The throng stepped forward; when a sunburnt son
Of Lymington, with brawny arms and brow
As massive as a bull's accosted us—
"Pray Sirs are you the gents who hither came
On yesterday and asked about a boat?"
"The same" we answered, "but we now propose
On economic grounds quite plain to you
To join the steamer and reject the boat".
"The day is fine" he urged "and if you take
A boat you can command it as you will.
Yon steamer casts its passengers ashore
At Yarmouth, but my merry craft is yours
To Alum Bay. The wind and tide this morn
Will sweep us there in two short hours, and you
Can quaff the breezes on the noble downs
Admire the pointed cliffs or dream for hours
Upon the yawning verge of Scratchell's bay".
The day was heavenly and the water shone
And Mrs Wright caught courage. In her eye
Her husband read her soul—"we go" he cried—
Eight shillings, is it not? The man said "yes".
And thus, the bargain closed, we spread our sails,
The boatman and his comrade grasped the oars
And I the helm; beacons of trees and pine
Stuck in the mud traced out a winding course
And this we followed. Half a little hour
Set us advancing on the emerald waves
Quite clear beyond the river, straight across,
For so the wind required, we scudded swift.
The steamer passed us, bearing at her stern
A stately yacht, with masts like slender spears
So tall, they seemed to scrape against the sky.
And ever and anon a note of joy
Jumped like a singing thrustle from the throat
Of Mrs Wright. Health was in every wave,
And I to give my muscles exercise
And by the friction of their fibres rub
All rust away from chest and ribs and arms
Seized a relinquished oar, and long I tugged
And then I steered again, and saw with joy
Our craft o'ertake and pass with conquering sweep

her canvassed sisters of the Solent sea.
We tacked and tacked, for so the wind decreed
While I with hand upon the helm took in
The boatman's hints and linked his facts to laws.
He knew the how, and I resolved the why
And through the light of principles discerned
A beauty in his acts unseen by him.
No sickness marred our pleasure: Mrs Wright
Drew forth defiant from her wicker pouch
A crust, which she disposed of in a way
That proved she liked it; and were sickness there
The agitation of the inner deeps
Affinities reversed and fortunes turned
In wrong directions would have doubtless made
A different picture far of Mrs Wright.
Safely arrived in lovely Alum Bay
We walked a narrow plank from boat to shore
For which the man who laid the plank received
The sum of sixpence, which with many thanks
As if it did exceed his normal gains
He pocketed amain, and we went on
Attracted by the colour of the cliffs
Which here stands vertical and tell a tale
Of dire commotion when the level beds
Of this fair isle were wildly tossed on end;
And to the thoughtful wanderer even now
Preach what the world was in the ages gone.
At times I bounded up the banded seams
Streaked with their purple green and red
And helped myself to specimens which broke
And crumbled in the pockets where they lay.
My scarf I cast upon the pebbled beach
Trusting no visitor to that fair strand
(For visitors were plentiful today)
Would stoop to peculation; now and then
I cast my wary eye upon the spot
Where the cloth rested; upward then my glance
Wandered and marked the courses of the flint
Running contorted through the massive chalk
Which manifestly shared the jerk which set
The neighbouring rocks on edge; a little cave

Worn by the lapping billows asked us in
We entered it, and heard the water plash
From roof to floor, the tangled weeds around
Its porch were gathered up by Mrs Wright.
Two maidens were beside us at the time
One stooped & raised a leaf, and holding high
The dripping shred, exclaimed in accents coarse
"What can she want with rubbish such as this?"
Meanwhile my anxious eye glanced back once more:
My plaid had disappeared! Speed stirred my limbs
And vengeance on the thief, if thief there were,
Took fire and burned determined in my heart.
I reached the place and found two yellow boys,
Yellow with dirt and tan, and at their sides
In contact with their proper filthy gear
I saw my scarf. I scowled upon the pair
And asked them why they dared to move my plaid
"To guard it for you" was the prompt reply.
"We found it stretched without an owner there
And to the owner we are ready now
To give it up". I scanned each urchin's face
On which the natural law or evil use
Had written scamp and scoundrel—"you young dogs!"
I cried in wrath, and turning then to Wright
"Is a policeman to be found?" I said
The rascals shivered, muttering once more
"We only meant to keep your wrapper safe".
I looked around, saw no policeman there
And with a frown which doubtless fell on them
As sunshine on the plants of Alum Bay
I left the varlets stretched upon the sand.

Upward we went, and where the man of stones
And shells and spar displays his island wares
I turned aside and sunk full half a crown
In geologic stuff. I wished to know
The way in which the stone was rendered hard.
There was a cataract on the seller's eye
On his right eye, which gave a lying look
To his whole countenance; but delayed
To draw from physical deformity

An inference to the prejudice of this man.
Alas he lied! The cataract on his soul
Was ten times worse than that upon his eye
He afterwards acknowledged that he lied
And with an effort I scooped out the truth
From his false lips. I bade his shed good bye
And faced the hill where my companions stood
Pondering my absence. From the Chine below
The broken music of a German band—
A ragged band came up the sunny hill.
And upon grassy platform cloths were spread
And mighty pies, and loaves, and ginger beer,
And picnic parties crowded round the food
"How capital"! I cried—they heard the word
And many a maiden with audacious lip
Dipped deeper in roses, jeered me and my joy
And asked me would I like to take a bit
Yet manifestly meant me not to take
Even if I liked it. Now we faced the hill,
The glorious down, close shaven, which extends
Its needle spurs into the western sea.
The way was steep, I bore the scarfs of all
And Wright in duty lent a helping arm
To his fair wife; my arm at once proferred she
Had found on trial that she must decline.
For at each step she trod upon her gown
Which therefore needed lifting, and for this
She claimed the freedom of the arm which hung
On mine, I loosed it, and jogged on alone.
And at the summit Mr Wright averred,
That he was blown. I stood on sturdy limbs
And measured the magnificent expanse
Of ocean, and the bending dome of sky
Which closed down on it, sweeping with a curve
Clear, definite as with a compass drawn
The far horizon beaded o'er with ships.
Along the ridge we walked, the crisping breeze
Was balm and cordial to our heated brows
To distant Freshwater our thoughts went on
Before our bodies. Images of stout
Reaming with foam, and Bass's sparkling ale

Raised locomotive wishes in our hearts
Which in those days when fairies scorn to lend
Their aid and seven leagued boots cannot be had
Were all in vain. Poor Mrs Wright oft sighed
And wished us there, and as each mocking ridge
Which promised when we reached it to reveal
The place on which our wearied hopes were fixed
Only deceived us, and poor soul quite spent
With cheeks all suffering from the ungentle kiss
Of scorching sunbeams oft and oft exclaimed
"Oh what a journey for us back again".
She thus forestalled an ill which never came:
For we got there, and with triumphant voice
I ordered fowl and ham. Poor Wright at first
Affirmed he could eat nothing, but one bite
Of that sweet fowl and that delicious ham
Awakened a capacity for food
Within him, which considering all his vows
Of absent appetite astonished me.
We fed right royally and quaffed our ale;
Our only drawback was that Mrs Wright
Adhered to bread and butter, eschewed wine
And lemonade, and every other draught
Which my remembrance taught me to suggest.
We fed right royally; and afterwards
We rode like princes back to Alum Bay.
Wright, as he smoked, and partly that he wished
To scan the landscape set himself on high
Beside the driver; "see" he quickly cried
"The house of Tennyson!"[6] I tried my best
To see the house, but beech and lime tree flung
Their clustering leaves between the house and road.
I saw a corner gleaming through the trees
It went—a second for a moment came
And that was all. No matter, 'twas a boon
To glance upon the corner of a house
Which holds a poet—One in whose clear mind
Burns a celestial coal, for ever bright.
No smoke, no glare, but smoke and glare condensed
To living fire which warms the hearts of men.
The air seemed fresher when we knew it was

The same that vivified his noble blood
Filled with the thought of him we settled down
And halted on the verge of Alum Bay
Here people thronged like pismires and a voice
Enquiring cried aloud to Mrs Wright
"Pray who's your hatter!" and the question spread
Like babbling echo, till a score of tongues
Thirsting for knowledge all enquired the same
And ere we found ourselves afloat once more
I marked a duskiness upon the face
Of our conductor, like the wreck of clouds
Which spreads at times confusion o'er the heavens
The man was muzzy from excess of beer
I kept my eye upon him, watching how
He shook his sail abroad and used his oar
His touch was prompt and sure: athwart the wrack
That marred his countenance his spirit saw
The work before him, and his ready hands
Were quick to execute his spirit's will.
"A nasty jump Sirs" he exclaimed as oft
The waves thumped at us through the sounding keel
Our sails at first shook idly: not a breath
Bellyed the canvass, but our oarsmen plied
Their oars and soon a stiff north easter sprung
Half angry on us from a clouded sky.—
Partially clouded, for while we in gloom
Scudded along, the cliffs of Alum Bay
Shone white and splendent in the smiling sun.
The wind augmented, and the waves at times
Butted our skiff like rams and made her pant
Through all her seams, while salt-spray from the prow
Caught by the wind fell over us in showers,
One half my plaid was swathed round Mrs Wright
An end around myself, who windward sat
And like a cliff received the rudest splash
Thus sheltering my companion. Wright was wrapped
In tartan plaid—his seamless countenance
Or from the strife within, or waves without
Imaged at intervals the tartan hue.
Eyeing the boatman he at times exclaimed
"You're in the waves again—I like the sea

But could dispense with this accursed see-saw!"
Though splashed and wet, with cheeks all hot and lips
All tender with the sunbeams and the brine
I felt unwonted strength within my frame.
I drank the breeze, and sang an inner song
To which the waves beat time: Could look aloft
And lift my heart on high; feel duty light
And glory in the vigour of a man.
Not as a week ago when smitten down
I crawled the earth, and felt with feeble hands
Across dispeptic tangle for the law
Which ought to guide the conduct of my life.
The law was now at hand, and forced to cope
With its demands, and render into deeds
The [peerless] aspirations of the soul.
The wind's eye dark and squally on we went
With sundry tackings—shifting to and fro.
And at each move the boatman with his flag—
Wiped the salt water from the flooded seat.
Once more we tracked the river's winding course
And landing safe we paid our men and clomb
The steep incline to the Commercial Inn.

A room where Wright and I the day before
Had sandwiches and beer received as now
The woolly carpet cut without regard
To symmetry of pattern bore the stains
Of scattered ink, while little oilskin prisms
Told us we sat where those in technic phrase
Called "bagmen" revel in commercial dreams.
A maiden with a mild voice and slender waist
And darkling eyes from which a radiance gleamed
Like Byron's lightning through the Alpine cloud
Asked us upstairs into a private room.
We went and had a tea the gods might share.
Wishing to pay the shot I rang the bell
But Wright forestalled me; yet the maiden came
And said "Oh Sir I thought I had seen
Your face before, but could not call to mind
How, when or where;—you lunched here yesterday".
"True", I responded gently "but as I

Have not forgotten you, it follows clear
That the impression which you made on me
Is deeper far alas! than mine on you".
The maiden bent her head and sweetly smiled
And rose and lilly rippled o'er her cheek
In waves of light while a more tender beam
Broke from the crystal of her shaded eye.
She softly spoke and hoped that I had found
The day a day of pleasure. I said "yes".
And as our voices thus began to flow
In one melodious current Mrs Wright
Damned the discourse by whispering she would tell
My friends how I had "flirted" with the girl!

Stunned by the threat: I bade the maid good bye
Drank the last light of her delicious eye
And halted at the bottom just to sip
The latest murmurs of her ruby lip.
Her image in my heart; her body where
The plane of the first lobby cuts the stair
And now the hostler yields the whip and rein
To Wright, who tickles Fanny's ribs again
A moment's hesitation—I am gone
And that dear maid may cogitate alone.
Alas! not so: the thought of Bagmen's arms
In the wrong place my jealous soul alarms
Oh happy Bagman—Oh unhappy me
The woe is mine—the waist remains to thee!

Oh soft and calm the saintly evening drooped
In silence o'er the earth—the world within
As warm and peaceful as the world without
Cradled in foliage lay the smiling fields
The soft green of the pastures gleaming through
Their sylvan frames of hazel and of elm.
The beanfields came to meet us with their balm
The tinted woodbine netted through the hedge
Poured out in sweetness all its floral soul
And when the twilight darkened into night
The knolls on either hand were like the sky
Studded with earthly stars: the grass was gemmed

With glow worms, one of which I knelt beside
And saw it like a little sun illume
The grass-blades near. And afterwards I sought
To make the nature of this wondrous thing
Called light, as far as science has explored
Its essence, manifest to Mrs Wright
Poor Wright was silent—afterwards I learned
That as we talked of ether and of waves
His stomach, shaken sadly by the sea,
Began to totter, and when he resigned
His charge at Mudeford he quite gave way.
For me I carried home a stack of force
A health, a hope, a happiness, a joy.
Which stamp the memory of this precious day
In big red letters on my grateful heart.

RI MS JT/2/7/355–372; RI MS JT/2/13b/853–60

1 There are two versions of this poem, and the first contains around 30 minor amendments. The second version was copied out, with a few changes, for Juliet Pollock on 18 July. See [1] July 1856, [draft], RI MS JT/8/2/58–67; and 18 July 1856, [Final fair copy], RI MS JT/8/2/68–73. The poem was written while Tyndall was spending a week's break at Muddeford, near Christchurch in Dorset, on the south coast, with his friends Richard Wright and Wright's wife. On 30 July they visited the Isle of Wight, described in this poem.

2 *Wright*: Richard Sears Wright (1829–92), English mathematician and teacher who taught engineering and surveying at Queenwood College from 1851.

3 *Allman*: not identified.

4 *Mrs Leary*: perhaps their landlady.

5 *In honour of the Queen*: perhaps in honour of Victoria becoming Queen on 20 June 1837.

6 *"The house of Tennyson!"*: Farringford, close to Freshwater Bay. At this point, Tyndall had not met Tennyson.

71 [What though the mountain breezes][1]
18 August 1856[2]

What though the mountain breezes
Do drive away the bile
It merely gives another room
For man is very vile

In vain in their sublimeness
The mountains lift their thrones
These heathens, sans the blindness
Will fret you to the bones!

RI MS JT/2/8/40–1; RI MS JT/2/13c/876

1 When two guides had tried to overcharge Tyndall and Huxley after taking them over the Wengen Alp, Tyndall wrote in his journal: 'I thought that a verse of Heber's might be parodied in somewhat the following fashion:' (RI MS JT/2/13c/876).

Heber's original reads as follows:

> From Greenland's icy mountains, from India's coral strand;
> Where Afric's sunny fountains roll down their golden sand:
> From many an ancient river, from many a palmy plain,
> They call us to deliver their land from error's chain.
>
> What though the spicy breezes blow soft o'er Ceylon's isle;
> Though every prospect pleases, and only man is vile?
> In vain with lavish kindness the gifts of God are strown;
> The heathen in his blindness bows down to wood and stone.
>
> Shall we, whose souls are lighted with wisdom from on high,
> Shall we to those benighted the lamp of life deny?
> Salvation! O salvation! The joyful sound proclaim,
> Till earth's remotest nation has learned Messiah's Name.
>
> Waft, waft, ye winds, His story, and you, ye waters, roll
> Till, like a sea of glory, it spreads from pole to pole:
> Till o'er our ransomed nature the Lamb for sinners slain,
> Redeemer, King, Creator, in bliss returns to reign.

2 Tyndall was at Grindelwald, with Thomas Huxley, on his first glacier explorations.

72 [The sea holds jubilee this sunny morn] 17 June 1861[1]

The sea holds jubilee this sunny morn
And I with heart content upon its verge[2]
Join in the laughter of the breaking waves.
And glad, right glad the sympathetic land,
Shaking her hazel tresses in her mirth
While all her copses tremble into song
The thickset trees which crowd the Undercliff,[3]
The scented woodbine on the neighbouring knoll,
The foxglove shaking all its purple bells,
And roses blushing mid the tender green,
All blend to form a bouquet for the sight;
But not for sight alone, for beauty sends
Its finer essence down into the heart.
Lady! my friend—thou surely wilt not frown,
If lingering here I miss that other joy
Of meeting thee and thine to-morrow night!
J.T. | Monday 17th June 1861.

John Tyndall to Juliet Pollock, 17 June 1861, RI MS JT/1/TYP/6/1978[4]
Typewritten transcript only

1 Tyndall went to the Isle of Wight on 16 June, returning on 19 June.
2 In the original version, written into Tyndall's journal the same day, the first two lines are slightly different:

> The sea is joyful on this sunny morn,
> While with heart content upon its verge

RI MS JT/2/10/283; RI MS JT/2/13c/1219

3 *Undercliff*: The Undercliff is a stretch of land on the south coast of the Isle of Wight, between Niton and Bonchurch.
4 See also letter 1788, TC7.

73 There was an unfortunate Divil August 1861[1]

There was an unfortunate Divil
Who wanted the view from the Riffel[2]
So tho' pathways were boggy
And atmosphere foggy
He clambered and climbed up the Riffel.

The way seemed amazing lontano
And tho' he went on piano piano
The rain & perspiring
Were drenching and tiring
and [not] the proverbial sano.

And sacré verflucht [maledetta]
And good round British oaths (which are better),
While not one "magnifique"
Or in growl or in squeak
Broke in on this Swiss Donner Wetter.

For Rosa[3] was still lachrymosa
Though known as puella formosa
And the great peak of Mattu[4]
Was buried in battu
And all nature venditio famosa.

So all things were chilly & clammy
To that Job might himself have cried D—me
Whilst alpenstocks battered
Boots stamped & tongues chattered
And no door but was creaky & slammy.

Beds, walls, floors are clammy & chilly,
And the "Night" the reverse quite of "Stilly",
Till this middle aged Divil
Who slept on the Riffel[5]
Had at length to get up, willy-nilly.

In this Tavern perfumed—not by [Rimmel]—
He glared for one speck of blau Himmel,

But from morning to night
The fog was as white
And as slow as a Postmeister's Schimmel.

With hobnails & uproar & bother
'Tis surely the Faulhorn's[6] own brother
And from chambers off
He could hear a great cough
As he set down some vessel or other.

He strove, this unfortunate Divil,
The tongue in his head to keep civil,
And scribbled his verses,
With deep, not loud, curses,
And then he went down from the Riffel.

August 1861

RI MS JT/3/21; Riffelberg Hotel Book, Matterhorn Museum archive. The latter enabled reading of some unclear words in the RI version.

1 Tyndall made the first ascent of the Weisshorn on 19 August 1861. He went on to Zermatt and up to the Riffelalp on 22 August, where he may have written this limerick before crossing the Théodule Pass to prospect the Matterhorn for a second time.
2 *Riffel*: the Riffelhorn, above Zermatt, gives a spectacular view of the glacier below and the peaks all around.
3 *Rosa*: Monte Rosa, the highest mountain in Switzerland, visible across the glacier from the Riffelhorn.
4 *Mattu*: The Matterhorn, across the valley beyond Zermatt, and still unclimbed at this point.
5 *Who slept at the Riffel*: there was, and still is, a hotel on the Riffelberg.
6 *Faulhorn's*: The Faulhorn is a peak near Grindelwald.

74 To the moon[1] 14 February 1863[2]

To the moon

1863 Feb. 14th

Say does the crimson of the drooping rose
When soft it falls upon delighted eyes
Close up those eyes against the glorious sun
Which gives all flowers their odours and their bloom?

Or does the song of lark and nightingale
Mingling at dawn along the Devon shore[3]
Make the full heart less fitted to enjoy
The grander music of the gleaming sea?

Is it not rather so, that when a love
So large as that which fills my soul for thee
Unlocks the doors, the smaller loves of earth
Troop in without disturbance to the great?
Dismiss thy fear; retract thy strong reproach
And bend thy beauty o'er me as of yore.—

Nor Bromine richly brown, nor Chlorine green—
Nor Aqueous Vapour[4] which the praying earth
Swings from her censers underneath thy beams,
Has ever caused my love to swerve from thee.

These are but melodies of minor note
Which mingle with that grander holier strain
My soul for ever sendeth to that heaven
Where thou dost reign, the Queen of all the Stars.

Dissolve those clouds, unpucker that fair brow,
Nor let thy lover for moment deem
The shock of worlds could move thy steadfast heart
Thou'rt bright once more,—come nearer then my love,—

Still nearer—stoop—a little lower—there!
I kiss thy silver cheek, Goodnight! Goodnight!

JT

Thus nobly mated we shall love through time—
Our time—& send the memory of our love
To other times; a torch to kindle trust
To burn up doubt, and give the sinking hearts
Of men reliance on the force of love.

I knew thee by thy eyes (J's)
Hamlet.

RI MS JT/8/2/1/74 (first 3 stanzas only); RI MS JT/1/TYP/6/2002

1 This poem actually consists of two sonnets followed by a 5-line fragment. In the typescript version, probably produced by Louisa, it appears immediately before poem 75, which is clearly to Juliet Pollock. This set of poems appear also to be to her. The fragment is followed by to 'thy eyes (J's)'. If so it is very revealing.
2 Tyndall was in London. He had not been very well for the previous week and spent much of it at Queenwood College.
3 *Devon shore*: in March 1861 Tyndall had undertaken a walking tour in Devon with Francis Galton and Vaughan Hawkins.
4 *Nor Aqueous Vapour*: Tyndall had given his Discourse 'On Radiation Through the Earth's Atmosphere' on 23 January.

75 [The queenly moon][1] March 28[2]

The queenly moon commands the plastic sea
Which rolls around the world its silvered brine
And thus on Sunday evening drawn by thee
I'll roll from woodless 'woods'[3] to 59.[4]

J.T.

March 28

RI MS JT/8/2/1/47, RI MS JT/1/TYP/6/2003

1 The queenly moon is probably Juliet Pollock.
2 It is possible that this poem dates to 1863, following poem 74. If so, Tyndall was probably in London. He had not been well for a while and had been uncharacteristically out of sorts emotionally, as Hirst had commented earlier in the month (Hirst Journal, RI MS JT/2/32c/1633).
3 'woodless "woods"' may be a reference to Tyndall's residence in London: 14 Waverley Place, St Johns Wood.
4 59 Montagu Square, home of the Pollocks.

76 From the Alps: a fragment/A morning on Alp Lusgen[1] 1881 (*Pall Mall Gazette*) and 1892 (*New Fragments*)

Pall Mall Gazette version:

The sun has cleared the hills, quenching the flush
Of orient crimson with excess of light.
The long grass quivers in the morning air
Without a sound; yet each particular blade
Hymns its own song, had we but ears to hear.
The hot rays smite us, but a rhythmic breeze
Keeps languor far away. Unslumbering,
The eye and soul take in the mighty scene.
The plummet from those heights must fall a mile,
To reach yon rounded mounds which seem so small.
They shrink in the embrace of vaster forms,
Though, placed amid the pomp of Cumbrian Fells,
These hillock crests would overtop them all.
Steep fall the meadows to the vale in slopes
Of freshest green, scarred by the humming streams,
And darkened here and there by clouds of pine.
Unplanted groves! whose pristine seeds, they say,
Were sown amid the flames of nascent stars.
How came ye thence and hither? Whence the craft
Which shook these gentian atoms into form,
And dyed them with azure deeper far
Than that of heaven itself on days serene?
What built these marigolds? What clothed these
knolls
With fiery bilberries? What gave the heath
Its purple blossoms and the rose its glow?
Ah weary head! the answer is abroad,
Buzzing through all the atmosphere of mind.
'Tis Evolution! East, West, North and South—
From droughty sage and spinster shrill we learn
'Twas Evolution! When that word has spread
Its magic to the limits of the world,
Till its reverberation thence becomes
A lullaby—how sweet 'twill be to doze
Over thy emptied cup of nectar'd sweets
Divine Philosophy!—To doze in peace.[2]

Low down, the yellow shingle of the Rhone
Hems in the scampering stream, which loops the
sand
In islands manifold—beyond, a town,
Whose plated domes flash back the solar blaze—
Large domes for town so small! But here erewhile
Unfurled itself the Jesuit oriflamme,
And souls were nurtured on the tonic creed
Of Loyola—grand creed! if only true.
Oh! sorrowing shade of him,[3] who preached through
life
Obedience to the Highest! could men find
That Highest much more[4] clear! Yon tonsured monk
Will lie and die obedient to a power
Which he deems highest, but which you deem
damned.
Not for a monk your message; but for men
With strength potential—leaders of the world
Who took the truth you preached to set them free.[5]

Scarred by a gorge, the vale beyond the town
Breaks into squares of yellow and of green—
Of rye and meadow. Through them winds the
road
Which opened to the hosts of conquering France
Lombardian plains—the Simplon Pass—
Flanked by the Lion Mountain to the left,
While to the right the mighty Fletschorn lifts
A beetling brow, and spreads abroad its snows.[6]
From one vast brain yon noble highway came;
"Let it be made," he said, and it was done.
In one vast brain was born the motive power
Which swept whole armies over heights unscaled,
And poured them, living cataracts, on the South.
Or was it force of faith, faith warranted
By antecedent deeds, that nerved these hosts
And made Napoleon's name a thunderbolt?
What is its value now? This man was called
"A mortal God!" Oh, shade before invoked,
You spoke of Might and Right; and many a shaft

Barbed with the sneer, "He preaches force—brute
force,"
Has rattled on your shield. But well you knew
Might, to be Might, must base itself on Right,
Or vanish evanescent as the deeds
Of France's Emperor. Reflect on this,
Ye temporary darlings of the crowd.
To-day ye may have peans in your ears;
To-morrow ye lie rotten, if your work
Lack that true core which gives to Right and Might
One meaning in the end.

J.T.[7]

'From the Alps: a fragment', *Pall Mall Gazette* (16 August 1881), p. 10 (signed J. T.)
Typewritten transcript only

New Fragments version:

The sun has cleared the peaks and quenched the flush
Of orient crimson with excess of light.
The tall grass quivers in the rhythmic air
Without a sound; yet each particular blade
Trembles in song, had we but ears to hear.
The hot rays smite us, but a quickening breeze
Keeps languor far away. Unslumbering,
The soul enlarged takes in the mighty scene.

The plummet from this height must sink afar
To reach yon rounded mounds which seem so small.
They shrink in the embrace of vaster forms,
Though, placed amid the pomp of Cumbrian Fells,
These hillock crests would overtop them all.
Steep fall the meadows to the vale in slopes
Of freshest green, scarred by the humming streams,
And flecked by spaces of primeval pine.
Unplanted groves! whose pristine seeds, they say,
Were sown amid the flames of nascent stars—
How came ye thence and hither? Whence the craft
Which shook these gentian atoms into form,

And dyed the flower with azure deeper far
Than that of heaven itself on days serene?
What built these marigolds? What clothed these
  knolls
With fiery whortle leaves? What gave the heath
Its purple bloom—the Alpine rose its glow?
Shew us the power which fills each tuft of grass
With sentient swarms?—the art transcending
  thought,
Which paints against the canvas of the eye
These crests sublime and pure, and then transmutes
The picture into worship? Science dumb—
Oh babbling Gnostic! cease to beat the air.
We yearn, and grope, and guess, but cannot know.

Low down, the yellow shingle of the Rhone
Hems in the scampering stream, which loops the
  sands
In islands manifold. Beyond, a town,
Whose burnished domes flash back the solar blaze—
Proud domes for town so small! But here erewhile
Unfurled itself the Jesuit oriflamme,
And souls were nurtured in the tonic creed
Of Loyola. Grand creed! if only true.
Oh! sorrowing shade of him,* who preached through
  life
Obedience to the Highest! could men find
That Highest much were clear! Yon tonsured monk
Will face the flames obedient to a power
Which he deems highest, but which you deem
  damned.

Cut by a gorge, the vale beyond the town
Breaks into squares of yellow and of green—
Of rye and meadow. Through them winds the road
Which opened to the hosts of conquering France
Lombardian plains—sky-touching Simplon Pass—
Flanked by the Lion Mountain to the left,
While to the right the mighty Fletschorn lifts
A beetling brow, and spreads abroad its snows.
Dom, Cervin—Weisshorn of the dazzling crown—

Ye splendours of the Alps! Can earth elsewhere
Bring forth a rival? Not the Indian chain,
Though shouldered higher o'er the standard sea,
Can front the eye with more majestic forms.

From one vast brain yon noble highway came;
'Let it be made,' he said, and it was done.
In one vast brain was born the motive power
Which swept whole armies over heights unscaled,
And poured them, living cataracts, on the South.
Or was it force of faith—faith warranted
By antecedent deeds, that nerved these hosts
And made Napoleon's name a thunderbolt?
What is its value now? This man was called
'A mortal God!' Oh, shade before invoked,
You spoke of Might and Right; and many a shaft
Barbed with the sneer, 'He preaches force—brute
 force,'
Has rattled on your shield. But well you knew
Might, to be Might, must base itself on Right,
Or vanish evanescent as the deeds
Of France's Emperor. Reflect on this,
Ye temporary darlings of the crowd.
To-day ye may have peans in your ears;
To-morrow ye lie rotten, if your work
Lack that true core which gives to Right and Might
One meaning in the end.

* Carlyle

'A morning on Alp Lusgen', *New Fragments* (London: Longmans, 1892), pp. 498–500; drafts are in RI MS JT/3/44 (see 76a–l).
Typewritten transcript only

1 There are two versions of this important poem, one almost certainly written in 1881 and the second in 1892, a year before Tyndall died. Thomas Carlyle had died on 5 February 1881, and this poem may be a direct response, honouring Carlyle, his view of the universe and his

morality. Tyndall went to the Alps on 17 June that year. He was not well initially, and the poem was probably written at Alp Lusgen in July. There are significant differences between the two versions. In particular the stanza 'Tis Evolution!' is missing from the later version. See Francis O'Gorman's article (1997) 'John Tyndall as Poet: Agnosticism and "A Morning on Alp Lusgen"', though O'Gorman clearly did not know of the *Pall Mall Gazette* version.

2 See RI MS JT/3/44 for the draft version for this stanza.

3 Unlike the 1892 version, Carlyle is not footnoted by Tyndall here. Perhaps, for a publication in 1881, he thought it obvious and unnecessary.

4 Tyndall crossed out 'more' and inserted 'were' (as in the 1892 version). This may be a misprint in *The Pall Mall Gazette*.

5 These three lines are not in the 1892 version. See RI MS JT/3/44 for the draft including this.

6 Five lines were added after this in the 1892 version.

7 Given the subject matter it is likely that many readers would have deduced the name of the author from these initials.

Select Bibliography

Alexander, Cecil Frances. 1850. *Hymns for Little Children*. London: Joseph Masters.

Baldwin, Melinda and Janet Browne (eds). 2016. *The Correspondence of John Tyndall*, vol. 2. Pittsburgh: Pittsburgh University Press.

Ballard, J. G. 1990. *The Atrocity Exhibition*. San Francisco: RE/Search Publications.

Bartlett, William V. 1995. 'Preaching Science: John Tyndall and the Rhetoric of Scientific Naturalism'. PhD thesis, Rutgers University.

Barton, Michael D., Janet Browne, Ken Corbett and Norman McMillan (eds). 2018. *The Correspondence of John Tyndall*, vol. 6. Pittsburgh: Pittsburgh University Press.

Barton, Ruth. 2018. *The X Club: Power and Authority in Victorian Science*. Chicago: Chicago University Press.

Barton, Ruth, Jeremiah Rankin and Michael S. Reidy (eds). 2017. *The Correspondence of John Tyndall*, vol. 3. Pittsburgh: Pittsburgh University Press.

Beer, Gillian. 2009. *Darwin's Plots: Evolutionary Narrative in Darwin, George Eliot and Nineteenth-Century Fiction*. 3rd ed. Cambridge: Cambridge University Press.

Brown, Daniel. 2013. *The Poetry of Victorian Scientists: Style, Science and Nonsense*. Cambridge: Cambridge University Press.

Browning, Robert. 1888. 'Men and Women'. In *The Poetical Works of Robert Browning*, vol. 4, 171–305. London: Smith, Elder and Co.

Cantor, Geoffrey. 2015. 'John Tyndall's Religion: A Fragment', *Notes and Records* 69: 125–39.

Cantor, Geoffrey and Gowan Dawson (eds). 2016. *The Correspondence of John Tyndall*, vol. 1. Pittsburgh: Pittsburgh University Press.

Choi, Tina Y. 2007. 'Forms of Closure: The First Law of Thermodynamics and Victorian Narrative', *English Literary History* 74: 301–33.

Clifford, William K. 1879. *Lectures and Essays*, ed. Leslie Stephen and Frederick Pollock. 2 vols. London: Macmillan.

Coleridge, Samuel Taylor. 1796. *Poems on Various Subjects*. London: C. G. and J. Robinson and Bristol: J. Cottle.

Dawson, Gowan and Sally Shuttleworth. 2003. 'Introduction: Science and Victorian Poetry', *Victorian Poetry* 41: 1–10.

DeArce, Miguel, Deirdre McGing and Norman McMillan. 2013–14. 'Two Forgotten Poems by John Tyndall (1841)', *Carloviana*.

DeYoung, Ursula. 2011. *A Vision of Modern Science: John Tyndall and the Role of the Scientist in Victorian Culture*. London: Palgrave Macmillan.

Elwick, James, Roland Jackson, Bernard Lightman and Michael S. Reidy (eds). 2016–. *The Correspondence of John Tyndall.* Pittsburgh: Pittsburgh University Press.

Eve, Arthur S. and Clarence H. Creasey. 1945. *Life and Work of John Tyndall*. London: Macmillan.

Finnegan, Diarmid, Roland Jackson and Nanna K. L. Kaalund (eds). 2019. *The Correspondence of John Tyndall*, vol. 7. Pittsburgh: Pittsburgh University Press.

Gold, Barri J. 2010. *ThermoPoetics: Energy in Victorian Literature and Science*. Cambridge, MA: MIT Press.

Harvey, George (trans.). 1814. *Ossian's Fingal: An Ancient Epic Poem*. London: Valpy.

Haugrud, Raychel A. 1970. 'Tyndall's Interest in Emerson', *American Literature* 41: 507–17.

Herapath, Jonathan and Emma Mason (eds). 2015. *Nineteenth-Century Poetry: Criticism and Debates*. London: Routledge.

Hesketh, Ian. 2019. 'Technologies of the Scientific Self: John Tyndall and His Journal', *Isis* 110: 460–82.

Hevly, Bruce. 1996. 'The Heroic Science of Glacier Motion', *Osiris*, 2nd series, 2: 66–86.

Holmes, John. 2012. '"The Poet of Science": How Scientists Read Their Tennyson', *Victorian Studies* 54: 655–78.

Holmes, John and Sharon Ruston (eds). 2017. *Nineteenth-Century British Literature and Science*. London: Routledge.

Huxley, Thomas H. 1894. 'Professor Tyndall', *The Nineteenth Century* 35: 1–11.

Illingworth, Sam. 2019. *A Sonnet to Science: Scientists and Their Poetry*. Manchester: Manchester University Press.

Jackson, Roland. 2018. *The Ascent of John Tyndall*. Oxford: Oxford University Press.

Jeans, William T. 1887. *Lives of the Electricians: Professors Tyndall, Wheatstone, and Morse*. London: Whittaker and Co.

Jenkins, Alice. 2007. *Space and the 'March of Mind': Literature and the Physical Sciences in Britain 1815–1850*. Oxford: Oxford University Press.

Lightman, Bernard. 2015. 'Fashioning the Victorian Man of Science: Tyndall's Shifting Strategies', *Journal of Dialectics of Nature* 38: 25–38.

Mackowiak, Jeffrey R. 2006. 'The Poetics of Mid-Victorian Scientific Materialism in the Writings of John Tyndall, W. K. Clifford and Others'. PhD thesis, University of Cambridge.

MacLeod, Roy and Peter Collins. 1981. *The Parliament of Science*. Northwood: Science Reviews.

McLeish, Tom. 2019. *The Poetry and Music of Science*. Oxford: Oxford University Press.

Mill, John Stuart. 1833. 'What is Poetry?', *Monthly Repository* 7: 60–70.

Milton, John. 1645. *Poems of Mr. John Milton, both English and Latin, Compos'd at Several Times*. London: Ruth Raworth for Humphrey Moseley.

Morrell, Jack and Arnold Thackray. 1981. *Gentlemen of Science: Early Years of the British Association for the Advancement of Science*. Oxford: Clarendon Press.

O'Gorman, Francis. 1997. 'John Tyndall as Poet: Agnosticism and "A Morning on Alp Lusgen"', *Review of English Studies* 48: 353–8.

Opie, Iona and Peter Opie (eds). 1952. *The Oxford Dictionary of Nursery Rhymes*. Oxford: Clarendon Press.

Opie, Iona and Peter Opie (eds). 1955. *The Oxford Nursery Rhyme Book*. Oxford: Clarendon Press.

Pratt-Smith, Stella. 2014. 'Boundaries of Perception: James Clerk Maxwell's Poetry of Self, Senses and Science'. In *James Clerk Maxwell: Perspectives on His Life and Work*, ed. Raymond Flood, Mark McCartney and Andrew Whitaker, 233–57. Oxford: Oxford University Press.

Quinney, Laura. 2009. *William Blake on Self and Soul*. Cambridge, MA: Harvard University Press.

Richards, Evelleen. 2017. *Darwin and the Making of Sexual Selection*. Chicago: Chicago University Press.

Ruskin, John. 1893. *The Queen of the Air*. New York: Maynard, Merrill and Co.

Ruskin, John. 1905. *The Eagle's Nest*. London: George Allen.

Russett, Cynthia E. 1989. *Sexual Science: The Victorian Construction of Womanhood*. Cambridge, MA: Harvard University Press.

Serres, Michel. 1982. *Hermes: Literature, Science, Philosophy*. Baltimore, MD: Johns Hopkins University Press.

Shelley, Percy Bysshe. 1840. 'A Defence of Poetry'. In *Essays, Letters from Abroad, Translations and Fragments*, ed. Mary Shelley, vol. 1, 1–57. London: Edward Moxon.

Sørensen, Majken J. 2015. 'Humorous Political Stunts: Speaking "Truth" to Power?', *European Journal of Humour Research* 1: 69–83.

Spencer, Herbert. 1861. *Education: Intellectual, Moral, and Physical*. New York: D. Appleton.

Spenser, Edmund. 1594. *Amoretti and Epithalamion*. London: William Ponsonby.

Sylvester, James J. 1870. *The Laws of Verse; or Principles of Versification*. London: Longmans, Green and Co.

Tate, Gregory. 2020. *Nineteenth-Century Poetry and the Physical Sciences: Poetical Matter*. London: Palgrave Macmillan.

Tennyson, Hallam. 1897. *Alfred Lord Tennyson: A Memoir*. 2 vols. London: Macmillan.

Trowbridge, Serena (ed.). 2018. *My Lady's Soul: The Poems of Elizabeth Eleanor Siddall*. Brighton: Victorian Secrets.

Tucker, Herbert F. 1996. 'When the Soul Had Hips: Six Animadversions on Psyche and Gender in Nineteenth-Century Poetry'. In *Sexualities in Victorian Britain*, ed. Andrew H. Miller and James Eli Adam, 157–86. Bloomington: Indiana University Press.

Turner, Frank. 1993. 'Ancient Materialism and Modern Science: Lucretius among the Victorians'. In *Contesting Cultural Authority: Essays in Victorian Intellectual Life*, 262–83. Cambridge: Cambridge University Press.

Tyndall, John. 1860. *The Glaciers of the Alps*. London: John Murray.

Tyndall, John. 1862. *Mountaineering in 1861*. London: Longman, Green, Longman, and Roberts.

Tyndall, John. 1863. *Heat Considered as a Mode of Motion*. London: Longman, Green, Longman, Roberts and Green.

[Tyndall, John]. 1864. 'Science and the Spirits', *The Reader* 102: 725–6.

Tyndall, John. 1865. 'The Constitution of the Universe', *Fortnightly Review* 3: 129–44.

Tyndall, John. 1867. *Sound: A Course of Eight Lectures Delivered at the Royal Institution of Great Britain*. London: Longmans.

Tyndall, John. 1870a. 'Scientific Use of the Imagination'. In *Essays on the Use and Limit of the Imagination in Science*, 1–51. London: Longmans.

Tyndall, John. 1870b. 'Scientific Limit of the Imagination'. In *Essays on the Use and Limit of the Imagination in Science*, 52–65. London: Longmans.

Tyndall, John. 1871. *Hours of Exercise in the Alps*. London: Longmans.

Tyndall, John. 1872a. 'On the Identity of Light and Radiant Heat', *Proceedings of the Royal Institution of Great Britain* 6: 417–21.

Tyndall, John. 1872b. *The Forms of Water in Clouds and Rivers, Ice and Glaciers*. London: King.

Tyndall, John. 1873. *Six Lectures on Light: Delivered in America in 1872–1873.* London: Longmans.

Tyndall, John. 1879. *Fragments of Science*. 6th ed. 2 vols. London: Longmans, Green and Co.

Tyndall, John. 1892. *New Fragments*. London: Longmans, Green and Co.

Tyndall, John. 1906. *Glaciers of the Alps & Mountaineering in 1861*. London: J. M. Dent and Sons.

Wordsworth, William. 1802. *Lyrical Ballads*, vol. 1. 3rd ed. London: Longman and Rees.

Subject Index

The subject index covers the introduction only, 'Poetry in context'.

Index of Names

The index of names covers the introduction and the poems.

CPSIA information can be obtained
at www.ICGtesting.com
Printed in the USA
JSHW021724160321
12559JS00002B/13

9 781787 359116